Nachhaltige Höhe Deutsche Messe AG Hannover
Verwaltungsgebäude

Sustainable Height Deutsche Messe AG Hannover
Administration Building

D1537582

Architekten / Architects: Herzog + Partner BDA, München
Thomas Herzog, Hanns Jörg Schrade
mit Roland Schneider

in Arbeitgemeinschaft mit
BKSP Projektpartner GmbH, Hannover

Mit Beiträgen von / Christof Bodenbach
With contributions by:

Richard A. Waters

Erhard Garske
Sailer Stepan und Partner GmbH, München

Gerhard Hausladen, Martin Többen
Ingenieurbüro Hausladen GmbH,
Kirchheim bei München

Herausgegeben von / Edited by: Thomas Herzog

Prestel München · London · New York

Inhalt / Contents

Ansicht vom Stadtteil Kronsberg aus,
im Vordergrund
neue Freianlagen zur EXPO 2000

View from Kronsberg, Hanover;
in the foreground, the new landscaped
open space for the EXPO 2000

Am Projekt Beteiligte / Persons and Firms Involved in the Project

Bauherr / Client
Deutsche Messe AG, Hannover
Standort / Location: Messegelände Hannover
Verantwortliches Mitglied des Vorstands /
Representative of the Managing Board:
Sepp D. Heckmann
Leitung Zentralbereich Technik / Director of Central Technical Office:
Dr. Rainar Herbertz

Architekten / Architects
Herzog + Partner BDA, München
Prof. Thomas Herzog, Hanns Jörg Schrade
Projektleitung / Project Architect: Roland Schneider
Mitarbeiter / Assistants:
Nico Kienzl, Christian Schätzke, Thomas Straub,
Brigitte Tacke, Stephanie Zierl
Inneneinrichtung / Interior Design:
Verena Herzog-Loibl

Duchführung und Abwicklung / Realization
BKSP Projektpartner GmbH, Hannover
Projektleitung / Project Supervisor: Ingo Brosch
Mitarbeiter / Assistants:
Wilfried Peters, Hans-Joachim Kaub, Peter Goral, Bärbel Degner

Tragwerksingenieure / Structural Engineers
Sailer Stepan und Partner GmbH, München
Kurt Stepan,
Dr.-Ing. Erhard Garske

**Ingenieure für Heizung, Lüftung, Kälte, Raumklima /
Engineers for Heating, Ventilation, Cooling and Indoor Climate**
Ingenieurbüro Hausladen GmbH, Kirchheim / München
Prof. Dr.-Ing. Gerhard Hausladen
Mitarbeiter / Assistants:
Martin Többen, Martin Kirschner, Ludwig Langer, Peter Maier
Bauleitung: Joachim Balser

Gebäudetechnik / Mechanical Services
Schmidt Reuter Partner
Ingenieurgesellschaft Hannover
Mitarbeiter / Assistants:
Udo Koslowsky, Dieter Schoppe, Wolf-Rüdiger Schönhoff,
Torsten Menge

**Aerodynamik, natürliche Belüftung – Energiesimulation /
Aerodynamic Studies, Natural Ventilation – Energy Simulation**
Design Flow Solutions, Arrington GB
Dr. Richard A. Waters, Prof. Phillip Jones, G. J. McDonald

Brandschutztechnisches Gutachten / Fire-Protection Consultants
Hosser, Hass + Partner, Braunschweig
Dr.-Ing. Rüdiger Hass

Geotechnisches Gutachten / Geotechnical Report
Dr.-Ing. Meihorst und Partner, Hannover
Karl-Heinz Mosbach

Vermessung / Surveying Services
Drecoll & von Berckefeldt & Wielitzek, Hannover

Fördertechnik / Lift Engineering
Hundt & Partner, Hannover

Schallschutz / Acoustic Control
Müller-BBM GmbH, Planegg bei München
Prof. K. H. Müller, G. Hilz

Seite 4/5
Fassaden-Ausschnitt: links Möding Argeton Fassade;
rechts Lüftungslamellen innerhalb der Metall/Glasfassade

pp. 4–5
Facade details: left, the Möding Argeton facade;
right, ventilation louvres
within the metal and glass facade

Luftaufnahme von Nordwesten: im Vordergrund
Eingangsbauwerk Nord, rechts Mitte Halle 18.
Die Änderung des baulichen Umfelds steht noch bevor,
um der Eingangssituation Transparenz zu geben

Aerial view from north-west: in the foreground,
the northern entrance structure; middle right, Hall 18.
Proposed changes to the surrounding developments
will lend the entrance situation a greater degree
of transparency

Ein bauliches Wahrzeichen

Christof Bodenbach

»Hannover ist eine Stadt, die sich dem Betrachter erst auf den zweiten Blick erschließt. Reich an natürlichen Grünflächen und im Besitz der weit über die Stadtgrenzen hinaus gerühmten barocken Gartenanlage Herrenhausen ist ihre Architektur vielleicht nicht so spektakulär, jedoch maßvoll und überschaubar.« (1)

Konzertierte Aktionen in Sachen Architektur finden in Hannover heutzutage vornehmlich im Zusammenhang mit zwei durchaus in Beziehung stehenden Ereignissen statt: Das eine ist die unmittelbar nach Ende des Zweiten Weltkrieges – notgedrungen als Alternative zum verlorenen Leipzig in der damaligen sowjetischen Besatzungszone – vollzogene Gründung der Deutschen Messe AG. Mehrmals im Jahr drängen nun deren Großveranstaltungen in die Stadt an der Leine. Das andere, geradezu als Initialzündung zu bezeichnende, ist die 1990 mit dem Willen zur langfristigen Weiterentwicklung des Messegeländes zusammenfallende Entscheidung, die erste Weltausstellung auf deutschem Boden im Jahr 2000 in Hannover stattfinden zu lassen. In der Folge wurde ein städtebaulicher Wettbewerb ausgelobt; der preisgekrönte Entwurf schlug vor, wesentliche Teile des Messegeländes in die EXPO 2000 zu integrieren. Man entwickelte einen Masterplan; das Büro Herzog + Partner erhielt den Auftrag, diesen im Hinblick auf eine verbesserte räumliche Gesamtsituation des Geländes und die natürliche Belichtung und Belüftung der einzelnen Hallen zu prüfen, ein Gesamtkonzept zu entwickeln und als erstes Projekt die in kurzer Zeit weithin bekannt gewordene Halle 26 sozusagen als Prototyp der »neuen Messe« zu bauen.

Ein weiteres bauliches Wahrzeichen der Messe – dem Motto der Weltausstellung »Mensch – Natur – Technik« zugeordnet – ist der schlanke, zwanziggeschossige Verwaltungsturm der Messegesellschaft. Unweit des Nordeinganges gelegen, weithin sichtbar, ergänzt der Solitär ein bestehendes Bürogebäude und ist das höchste Haus Hannovers. Der Bau wurde von Thomas Herzog, Hanns Jörg Schrade und Mitarbeitern im Hinblick auf hohe Arbeitsplatzqualität und den innovativen Einsatz von Umweltenergie entworfen; Behaglichkeit und niedriger Energieverbrauch waren die Parameter. Die beengte Grundstückssituation war Anlaß, ein hohes Gebäude zu konzipieren. Städtebaulich und architektonisch orientiert sich der Turm über seine Diagonale: Die zurückgesetzte, dreigeschossige Eingangshalle ist voll verglast und verklammert so den (öffentlichen) Vorplatz des Nordeinganges mit dem (halböffentlichen) Grünbereich des Messegeländes. Messe und Stadt treten gleichsam in Verbindung. Die angestrebte Neuordnung des Nordeingangs ist derzeit jedoch noch nicht Realität.

Das städtebaulich-räumliche Grundkonzept mit seiner diagonalen Orientierung zum Grünraum und die Transparenz im Eingangsbereich ist daher Option für die Zukunft, deren baldige Umsetzung dringend zu wünschen ist, weil erst die Verwirklichung dieser architektonischen Kernidee des Entwurfes die Proportion des Baukörpers und die großzügige Weite des Zugangs voll zur Wirkung bringen wird.

»Thomas Herzog verbindet bei seiner Architektur technisch-konstruktives Können mit einem ausgeprägten Verantwortungsbewußtsein für die gebaute Umwelt«, heißt es im Lexikon der Architektur des 20. Jahrhunderts (2). Er begibt sich dabei auf Spurensuche und wird fündig: in der Natur, in anderen Kulturkreisen, in Industriezweigen, die nichts mit dem Bauen zu tun haben.

So erinnert das Lüftungskonzept des Hannoveraner Verwaltungsturmes an die komplexen, traditionell ohne Mechanik auskommenden Klimatisierungssysteme im Iran oder im extrem heißen arabischen Raum.

Architektur ist für den Münchner eben nicht nur Ästhetik. »Es geht im ganz traditionellen Sinne nach wie vor um alle drei klassischen Kategorien, die Vitruv benannt hat: die funktionale Tauglichkeit der Bauten, die richtige Technik des Bauens und die Schönheit der Gebäude.« (3)

Thomas Herzog ist einer der ganz wenigen echten (Bau-)Forscher unter Deutschlands Architekten – und Architekturhochschullehrern. Er hat das Bauen als ganzes im Blick, er arbeitet in Akademie und Werkstatt zugleich. Auf die Kultur des Machens legt er großen Wert.

»Von Anbeginn galten die Forschungen Herzogs der Leistungsfähigkeit hochentwickelter und innovativer Baukonstruktionen« (4); er selbst spricht von dem Ziel der »gestalterisch überzeugenden Leistungsform«. Ein schönes Beispiel für die Zähigkeit und Kontinuität des »Materialforschers« ist die Fassadenbekleidung der beiden am gläsernen Büroturm angelagerten Erschließungstürme. Sie geht auf seit 1978 betriebene Studien leichter, nichttragender Außenwandkonstruktionen zurück und ist die optimierte Weiterentwicklung eines 1984 erstmals eingesetzten Systems aus vorgehängten, hinterlüfteten Ziegelplatten samt Unterkonstruktion, das als Wetterschutz für bestehende und neue Bauten vor außenliegender Wärmedämmung zu montieren ist. Man muß die Architektur nicht jeden Montag neu erfinden.

Hannovers Architektur ist vielleicht nicht so spektakulär, jedoch maßvoll und überschaubar – wie die Häuser Thomas Herzogs, die auch lange nach dem Ende der Weltausstellung an der Leine am 31. Oktober 2000 Bestand haben werden.

(1) Architektur in Hannover seit 1900, München 1981
(2) Lexikon der Architektur des 20. Jahrhunderts, 2. Aufl., Ostfildern 1998, Seite 159
(3) Der Architekt 5 / 99, Seite 43
(4) Lexikon der Architektur des 20. Jahrhunderts, 2. Aufl., Ostfildern 1998, Seite 158

A Constructional Landmark

Christof Bodenbach

"Hanover is a city that reveals itself to the observer only at second glance. Although it possesses a wealth of natural open spaces as well as the famous Baroque gardens of Herrenhausen, its architecture is perhaps less spectacular and is distinguished instead by qualities such as clarity and moderation."(1)

Today, any concerted action in the realm of architecture in Hanover is likely to take place in conjunction with one of two related events. The first occurred immediately after the Second World War, when a new German trade fair organization, the Deutsche Messe AG, was founded as a necessary alternative to the corresponding institution in Leipzig, which at that time was lost in the Soviet zone of occupation. Numerous important functions are now staged every year at the trade fair site in Hanover on the River Leine. The second important event – something in the nature of a booster rocket, so to speak – was a decision taken in 1990 that expressed the will to continue the development of the trade fair site and to mount the first world exhibition ever to be staged in Germany: in Hanover in the year 2000. Following this decision, an urban planning competition was held. The prize-winning scheme proposed the incorporation of large sections of the trade fair site into the area foreseen for the EXPO 2000. A master plan was drawn up. The architects Herzog + Partner were commissioned to examine the plan in the context of improving overall spatial conditions on the site as well as the natural lighting and ventilation of the individual halls; to draw up an overall concept; and to design and construct the first project, Hall 26, as a prototype for the "new trade fair". Within a short time, Hall 26, has become a widely acclaimed architectural object.

A further constructional landmark of the trade fair site, a building that gives expression to the EXPO 2000 motto, "Man – Nature – Technology", is the slender 20-storey administration tower for the trade fair organization. Located near the northern entrance to the site and visible from afar, this singular free-standing structure is an extension of an existing office block and is the tallest building in Hanover. Designed by Thomas Herzog, Hanns Jörg Schrade and their team, it reflects the conditions of the brief, which required high-quality workplaces and an innovative exploitation of environmentally friendly forms of energy. In other words, the design parameters were working comfort and low energy consumption. The great height of the building was determined by the tight site conditions. Architecturally and in terms of the urban planning, the tower is oriented on the diagonal: the recessed, three-storey entrance hall is fully glazed and thus creates a link between the (public) forecourt at the northern point of access and the (semi-public) landscaped area of the trade fair site. In other words, the structure connects the city with its trade fair.

"In his architecture, Thomas Herzog unites technical and constructional skills with a strong sense of responsibility for the built environment."(2) He sets out on a quest and makes a number of discoveries on the way – in nature, in other cultures and in branches of industry that have nothing to do with building.

The ventilation concept for the Hanover tower, for example, is reminiscent of the complex, traditional, non-mechanical air-conditioning systems to be found in Iran and in Arab countries with extremely hot climates.

For this Munich architect, architecture is not just a matter of aesthetics. "In the traditional sense of the word, he is concerned with all three classical categories described by Vitruvius: functional efficiency, appropriate constructional techniques, and the beauty of a building."(3)

Thomas Herzog is one of the very few true (constructional) scientists among German architects – and indeed among university teachers of architecture. He comprehends building in its entirety. His sphere of activity is the academy and the workshop. He attaches great importance to the culture of doing things.

"From the very beginning, Herzog has addressed himself in his research work to the efficiency of highly developed, innovative forms of construction."(4) He describes his goal as "efficient form, convincingly designed". A good example of the tenacity and perseverance of this "researcher of materials" may be found in the facade cladding to the two core structures flanking the central glazed office tower in Hanover. The facings are based on studies of light-weight, non-load-bearing forms of external wall construction, which Herzog has pursued since 1978. The cladding to the tower in Hanover represents an optimized development of a system first used in Lohhof near Munich in 1984. It consists of a form of construction using clay tiles fixed to a supporting structure and with a ventilated cavity to the rear. The system provides weather protection for existing and new buildings and is erected over an external layer of thermal insulation. Architecture does not have to be reinvented every Monday.

Hanover's architecture may not be particularly spectacular. It is, however, distinguished by a quality of clarity and moderation – like Thomas Herzog's buildings, which will endure long after the World Exposition on the River Leine closes its gates on 31 October 2000.

(1) Architektur in Hannover seit 1900, Callwey, Munich, 1981
(2) Lexikon der Architektur des 20. Jahrhunderts, Hatje, Ostfildern, 2nd ed. 1998, p. 159
(3) Der Architekt 5/99, p. 43
(4) Lexikon der Architektur des 20. Jahrhunderts, Hatje, Ostfildern, 2nd ed. 1998, p. 158

Architektur und Gebäudekonzept

Thomas Herzog

Architecture and Constructional Concept

Aufgabe

Nach vorausgegangenen Untersuchungen zu Standortalternativen für ein Erweiterungsgebäude ihrer Verwaltung beauftragte uns die Deutsche Messe AG Hannover mit Entwurf, Planung und Realisierung eines Neubaus. Hohe Qualität der Arbeitsplätze und innovativer Einsatz von Umweltenergie für den Betrieb des neuen Gebäudes wurden erwartet.

Grundstück

Das Baugrundstück liegt unmittelbar hinter dem Messeeingang Nord und dem bestehenden Verwaltungsgebäude. Südlich angrenzend befindet sich die Halle 18. Die Ausdehnung des Grundstückes in Nord-Süd-Richtung entspricht dem Abstand zwischen diesen Bauten und beträgt 40 m.

Vor der Bauzeit befand sich auf dem Grundstück ein zweigeschossiger Südflügel mit Vorstandsräumen, der abgerissen wurde.

Im Osten bildet die Haupterschließungsstraße des nördlichen Messegeländes, die Mittelallee, die Begrenzung. Das Gelände fällt von dort nach Westen um ca. 1,80 m, von Norden nach Süden ca. 0,40 m.

Baukörper und Konstruktion

Die beengte Grundstückssituation war Anlaß, ein hohes Gebäude zu entwickeln. Im Grundriß ist der Baukörper in einen quadratischen Büroturm mit einer Seitenlänge von ca. 24 m x 24 m und zwei nordöstlich und südwestlich angelagerte Erschließungstürme gegliedert. So entstanden geschoßweise Nutzungseinheiten von nicht mehr als ca. 400 m². wodurch erhöhte Bauauflagen vermieden wurden. In Verbindung mit den diagonal gegenüberliegenden Treppenhäusern ergibt sich eine für den Personenschutz ideale Fluchtwegsituation.

Räumlich orientiert sich das Gebäude – was architektonisch von zentraler Bedeutung ist – über seine Diagonale vom Nordeingang aus in Richtung des großen Grünbereichs im Messegelände. Der durch die zurückgesetzte Fassade wettergeschützte südliche Zugangsbereich dient als Vorfahrt.

Brief

After an investigation of various alternative locations for an extension to their administration building, the Deutsche Messe AG in Hanover entrusted us with the design, planning and realization of a new building on the trade fair site in that city. The brief required the design of top-quality workplaces and an innovative use of environmentally friendly forms of energy for the operation of the new building.

Site

The site is located in the immediate vicinity of the northern entrance to the trade fair site and the existing administration building. Adjoining the development to the south is Hall 18. The site extends over a length of 40 metres in a north-south direction between these two structures.

Before the commencement of construction work, the site was occupied by the two-storey southern wing of the administration building, which contained rooms for the board of management. This wing was demolished to make space for the new structure.

The eastern boundary of the site is formed by the central avenue, which represents the main circulation route of the northern part of the trade fair grounds. The site slopes down from there to the west by roughly 1.80 metres. From north to south, the difference in level is about 0.40 metres.

Building volume and form of construction

The decision in favour of a high-rise building was the outcome of the tight site conditions. The layout is articulated into a square office tower roughly 24 x 24 metres on plan and two "core" or access structures to the northeast and south-west. This resulted in single-storey functional units of not more than about 400 square metres in area, which in turn meant that it was possible to avoid more stringent building regulations for this type of building. By setting the staircases

Lageplan des gesamten EXPO-Geländes: oben im roten Kreis das Verwaltungsgebäude am Eingang Nord, rundum das Messegelände mit den Pavillons der Weltausstellung; rechts außen die Stadtbahn-Station Brüsseler Straße; links außen die ICE-Bahnstrecke mit dem Bahnhof Hannover-Laatzen

Overall EXPO-site plan: the administration building near the northern entrance is at the top in the red circle, with the trade fair site and the pavilions for the World Exposition laid out around it; right: Brüsseler Strasse urban railway station; extreme left: the intercity-express rail route with Hanover-Laatzen Station

Das Gebäude hat 20 Vollgeschosse;
sie bestehen aus:

- einer zurückgesetzten, über drei Geschosse reichenden Eingangshalle,
- 14 Bürogeschossen (Regelgeschosse),
- einer Vorstandsetage,
- der sogenannten »Hermes-Lounge«,
- einem Technikgeschoß.

Hinzu kommt ein Untergeschoß.

diagonally opposite each other, ideal fire-safety conditions were created for users in terms of escape routes.

Of central importance to the architectural design is the transparent volume of the building and its spatial orientation on the diagonal from the northern site entrance to the large landscaped open space to the south-east. The southern access area, which

Die einzelnen Geschosse können individuell unterschiedlich aufgeteilt werden. Je nach Bedarf können je Geschoß 15 bis 20 Büroarbeitsplätze mit Fassadenanschluß als Großraum-, Kombi- oder Zellenbüro eingerichtet werden. Für die Büroorganisation, die technische Infrastruktur und insbesondere für die Behaglichkeit ist für jeden Arbeitsplatz etwa die gleiche Qualität erreichbar. Die Mittelzone der Büroeinheiten ist als Gemeinschaftsfläche genutzt.

Die komplett verglaste neue Eingangshalle, die im Zuge einer möglichen Neugestaltung des Messe-Nordeingangs die Haupterschließung der Messeverwaltung darstellen soll, hat Eingänge von Westen und Süden.

Unter der Eingangsebene befindet sich ein Untergeschoß mit Technikräumen. Die einzelnen Geschosse des alten Verwaltungsgebäudes sind durch einen Übergang an den Neubau angebunden. Der mittige Büroturm hat eine maximale Höhe von 67 m bis zur Dachebene, der Fußboden des höchstgelegenen Aufenthaltsraumes liegt knapp unterhalb der 60 m-Grenze.

Die beiden außenliegenden Erschließungstürme sind so situiert und proportioniert, daß sie die Süd- und Ostseite des Gebäudes im Anteil seiner Glasflächen reduzieren bzw. es verschatten, was angesichts der Vollverglasung des Büroteils im Hinblick auf Überhitzungs- und Blendungsprobleme von besonderer Bedeutung ist.

Der nordöstliche Erschließungsturm dient im wesentlichen der Vertikalerschließung durch Personenaufzüge und eine Treppe. Im südwestlichen Erschließungsturm befinden sich neben einer Treppe und dem Feuerwehr- bzw. Lastenaufzug die Sanitärräume.

Beide Treppenräume führen bis auf die Dachebene (+ 66,5 m), der nordöstliche zusätzlich bis ins Untergeschoß; die Personenaufzüge im Nordostkern bis auf die oberste Ebene mit Aufenthaltsräumen (»Hermes-Lounge«, + 58,3 m), der Feuerwehraufzug bis in das Technikgeschoß (+ 62,3 m). Der nordöstliche Kern hat eine Gesamthöhe von 85 m

is protected against the weather by setting back the facade, serves as the vehicle approach route.

The building has 20 full storeys, comprising
• a recessed entrance hall three storeys high
• 14 office storeys (standard floors)
• an executive floor with board rooms
• the "Hermes Lounge"
• a mechanical services storey.

The individual floors can be divided up in different ways. Depending on requirements, between 15 and 20 office workplaces can be located next to the facade on each floor. The offices can be in the form of open-plan, combination or individual unit spaces. It was possible to achieve virtually the same level of quality for all workplaces especially in terms of comfort, but also in respect of organization and the technical infrastructure. The central zone of each office storey is used for communal purposes.

The fully glazed new entrance hall – accessible from the west and south – is foreseen as the main point of access to the trade fair administration in the event of a redesign of the northern entrance to the site.

Beneath the entrance level is a basement with spaces for mechanical services. A linking tract connects the individual floors of the existing administration building to the new structure. The central office tower has a maximum height of 67 metres up to roof level. The floor level of the uppermost occupied space is just below the 60-metre limit. The two outer core structures are laid out and dimensioned in such a way that they reduce or shade the areas of glazing to the south and east faces of the building. In view of the fully glazed office facades, this is an important factor in terms of overheating and glare.

The north-east core serves principally as a means of vertical circulation, containing passenger lifts and a staircase. The south-west core houses the sanitary facilities as well as a further staircase and a firefighting/goods lift.

Both staircases lead up to roof level (+ 66.5 m). The north-east staircase also pro-

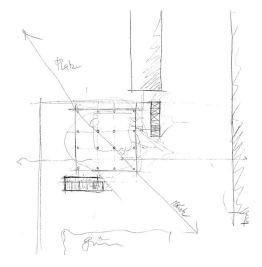

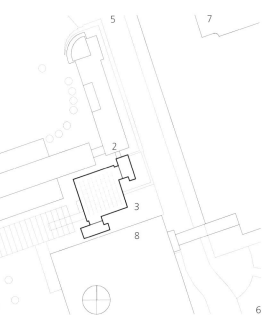

ohne Aufbauten (Lüftungsturm, Antennen), der südwestliche ist 70 m hoch. Die im Nordost-Erschließungsturm, oberhalb der Dachebene liegenden reinen Technikgeschosse werden intern über eine Wendeltreppe erschlossen.

Das Tragwerk für das neue Verwaltungsgebäude ist ein Stahlbetonskelettsystem. Die Ortbetondecken werden von 16 Stützen getragen, deren Abstand 6,30 m bzw. 7,80 m beträgt. Die aussteifenden Erschließungstürme bestehen aus 40 cm starken Stahlbetonwänden. Der auf dem Nordkern aufgesetzte Turm ist als Stahlkonstruktion ausgeführt.

Fassaden, thermisches Konzept und Lüftungskonzept

Die Bekleidung der Erschließungstürme erfolgte durch eine vorgehängte, hinterlüftete Ziegelfassade nach dem System Möding Argeton auf Aluminium-Unterkonstruktion. Das helle Perlgau ist die Eigenfarbe des keramischen Scherbens, also nicht oberflächiger Farbauftrag; diese Farbgebung wurde speziell für das Messehochhaus neu entwickelt. Erstmals sind Fassadenplatten mit Rillen angewendet, was zwei Vorteile bietet: Die horizontalen Rillen bremsen bei Regen das Fassadenwasser, das bei hohen Windgeschwindigkeiten im oberen Randbereich an der Fassade hochgetrieben wird, und sie vermindern Spannungsspitzen beim Herstellungsprozeß. Die optische Betonung der Horizontalen wird durch besonders schmale Vertikalfugen zusätzlich hervorgehoben.

Die Doppelfassade, welche die Büroflächen umhüllt, enthält in beiden Ebenen Zwei-Scheiben-Isolierglas, wobei in der äußeren Ebene Weißglas eingebaut wurde, um erhöhte Transparenz zu erreichen und Farbveränderungen bei der Sicht nach draußen gering zu halten. Die Fassaden sind innen aus Holz und Glas mit integriertem Brüstungskanal, außen aus Stahl und Glas in Pfosten/Riegel-Bauweise mit extrem schmalem Alu-Abdeckprofil konstruiert.

vides access to the basement. The passenger lifts in the north-east core serve the topmost level in which there are occupied spaces (Hermes Lounge, + 58.3 m). The firefighting lift goes up to the services storey (+ 62.3 m). The north-east core has an overall height of 85 metres, excluding roof structures such as the ventilation tower, aerials, etc. In this core, the storeys above the tower roof level used exclusively for services are reached via an internal spiral staircase. The southwest core has an overall height of 70 metres.

A reinforced concrete skeleton frame system was used for the load-bearing structure of the new administration building. The in-situ concrete slabs are supported by 16 columns at 6.30 and 7.80 m centres. The reinforced concrete walls to the stiffening cores are 40 centimetres thick. The northern core is surmounted by a steel tower structure.

Facades, and Thermal and Ventilation Concepts

The core towers are clad externally with a clay-tile curtain wall construction based on the Möding Argeton system. The cladding is fixed to an aluminium supporting structure and is ventilated by a cavity to the rear. The pale pearl-grey colour of the tiles, which was specially developed for the trade fair tower, is the natural colour of the ceramic material. In other words, it is not a surface pigment. Facing slabs with horizontal grooves were used here for the first time. The grooves have the advantage that they retard the flow of rainwater over the facade and thus prevent the water being driven upwards by high winds at the top of the building. The grooves also reduce extreme stresses in the tiles during the manufacturing process. The visual emphasis placed on the horizontal lines is accentuated by the especially narrow vertical joints.

Both skins of the two-layer facade around the offices are in double glazing. Flint glass was used in the outer skin to ensure a

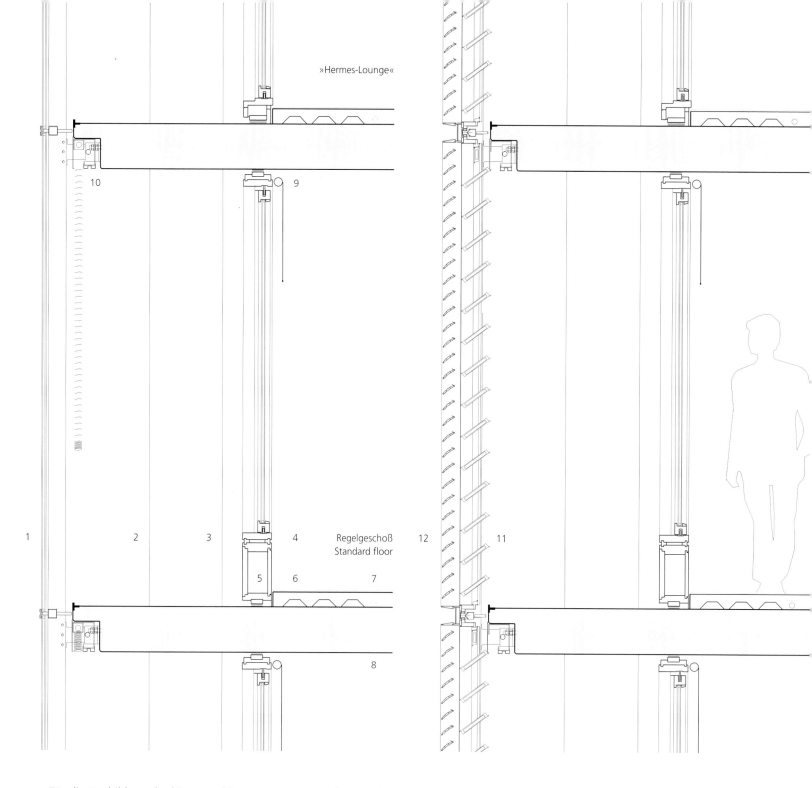

»Hermes-Lounge«

1 2 3 4 Regelgeschoß
Standard floor
5 6 7

8

12 11

10 9

Für die Ausbildung der hier gewählten, horizontal durchlaufenden, sogenannten »Korridorfassade« – einer speziellen Form von Doppelfassade – sprachen wesentliche Argumente:

• Da die äußere Hülle nur Wetterschutzfunktionen hat und geometrisch einfach und konstruktiv auf wenige sehr resistente Elemente reduziert ist, kann sie Zug um Zug dem Tragwerk folgend montiert werden. So kann die innere, technisch und funktional erheblich aufwendigere Fassade wetterunabhängig als Teil des Innenbaus unter erheblich günstigeren Bedingungen montiert werden.

• Der umlaufende Korridor wirkt als großräumiger Luftkanal, der Zuluft über druckabhängig steuerbare Lamellen in der äuße-

greater degree of transparency and to minimize colour distortion in the view out from the interior. The inner skin of the double facade is a wood-and-glass construction, with service ducts integrated into the apron panels beneath the windows. The outer skin is in a steel post-and-rail form of construction.

The use of this special double-facade construction – or horizontally continuous "corridor facade" – offers a number of important advantages.

• Since the external skin has the sole function of providing protection against the weather and is of a geometrically simple design with a construction reduced to only a few very resistant elements, it can be assembled step by step following the erection of the load-bearing structure. As a

Schnitte durch die Doppelfassade, Maßstab 1:25,
links Festverglasung, rechts Lamellenfeld

1 Metall/Glas-Fassade
   Pfosten und Riegel aus Stahlhohlprofilen,
   Wärmeschutzverglasung
2 Zwischenraum Doppelfassade
3 Stahlbetontragwerks-Stütze
4 Holz/Glas-Fassade
   mit Schiebe-Fenstertüren zur natürlichen Lüftung,
   Wärmeschutzverglasung
5 Zuluft-Kanal mechanische Lüftung
6 Unterflurkanal
   für Elektro- und Kommunikationstechnik
7 Heiz- und Kühlleitungen in Estrich 10 cm
   (Einzelheiten Seite 56)
8 Stahlbetondecke
9 Blendschutzrollo
10 Sonnenschutz-Jalousien
11 Glaslamellen, beweglich,
   Öffnungsstellung automatisch gesteuert,
   Wärmeschutzverglasung
12 Wetterschutzlamellen

Sections through two-layer facade scale 1:25;
left: fixed glazing; right: louvre strip

1 Metal and glass facade:
   hollow steel section posts and rails
   with aluminium cover strips
   low-E glazing – flint glass
2 Intermediate space in two-layer facade – air corridor
3 Reinforced concrete column
4 Wood and glass facade with sliding
   doors for natural ventilation; low-E glass
5 Air-supply duct for mechanical ventilation
6 Subfloor conduit for electrical
   and communications technology
7 Heating and cooling runs in 10 cm screed
   (for details, see p. 56)
8 Reinforced concrete floor slab
9 Anti-glare blind
10 Sunblind
11 Adjustable glass louvres with automatic setting:
   low-E glass
12 Protective louvre construction

ren Fassadenebene erhält und über Fenster die Büroräume mit Außenluft versorgt. Die Anordnung der Lamellenfelder wurde in aufwendigen Windkanalversuchen und Simulationen ermittelt.

• Eine thermische Pufferzone umhüllt den eigentlichen Nutzflächenbereich der Büroetagen, was energetisch günstig ist und ein gutes Strahlungsmilieu und damit hohen thermischen Komfort für Nutzer im Innenraum bietet.

• Hinter der äußeren Glasebene, im wind- und wettergeschützten Bereich, kann ein veränderbarer Sonnenschutz, in einfacher Form und für Wartung gut zugänglich, angeordnet werden.

• Die Verglasung der Etagen ist bis zum Boden möglich, was für die Tageslichtnutzung günstig und für die großzügige Wirkung der Räume entscheidend ist. Bei den Nutzern entstehen dabei wegen der auskragenden Decken keine Höhenängste.

• Die auskragende Decke kann als horizontale Brandüberschlagsschürze ausgebildet werden, ohne daß thermische Abtrennung erforderlich wäre.

• Die im Zwischenraum stehenden Stützen beeinträchtigen nicht die eigentlichen Büroflächen.

Beheizen und Kühlen basieren maßgeblich auf der thermischen Aktivierung der Gebäudemassen. Die massiven, unverkleideten Geschoßdecken mit Verbundestrich dienen als Speicher für das im Estrich verlegte Heiz- und Kühlsystem (Bauteilheizung und -kühlung oder auch »Thermoaktive Decke«), das zusammen mit der gewählten Lüftung ein optimales, individuell beeinflußbares Innenraumklima erzeugt. Die internen Wärmequellen (Personen, Geräte, Leuchten) reichen weitgehend aus, um das Gebäude in der Zeit, da es benutzt wird, zu heizen.

Im Sommer einfallende solare Strahlungswärme wird über die hohen Luftvolumenströme zwischen innerer und äußerer

result, the inner facade layer, which is technically and functionally far more elaborate, can be installed independently of weather conditions and under much more favourable circumstances as part of the fitting out of the interior.

• The peripheral corridor functions as a large-volume ventilation duct. Depending on pressure conditions, automatically controlled louvres in the outer layer of the facade admit external air into this space. From here, the air enters the offices via openable windows. The location of the bays of louvres was determined on the basis of elaborate wind-tunnel tests and simulations.

• The office storeys used by the staff are enclosed within a thermal buffer zone. This form of construction helps to cut energy consumption and also ensures a pleasant working environment by reducing insolation and providing users with a high degree of indoor thermal comfort.

• Adjustable sunshading can be installed in a simple form in the space behind the outer layer of glazing, where it is accessible for maintenance and protected against the weather.

• The glazing to the various storeys can extend down to the floor. This guarantees a good level of daylight internally and also creates a sense of ample space. The cantilevered floor slabs ensure that users do not experience any sense of vertigo as a result of the great height of the tower.

• The cantilevered sections of the floor slabs can be constructed as fire-breaks without the thermal separation that would normally be required.

• The columns in the intermediate corridor space do not obstruct the actual office areas.

Heating and cooling are based primarily on the thermal activation of the solid volumes of the building. The unclad floor slabs with monolithic screeds function as thermal

Schnitt aa (Schnittebene siehe Seite 22 bis 25),
Maßstab 1:500

1 Gründung
2 Untergeschoß
3 Eingangshalle
4 Bürogeschosse
5 »Hermes-Lounge«
6 Technikgeschoß
7 Lüftungsschacht
8 Erschließungsflur, Aufzüge
9 Doppelfassade
10 Aufzugsmaschinenraum
11 Rotations-Wärmetauscher
12 Lüftungstechnik
13 Technikräume
14 Lüftungsturm

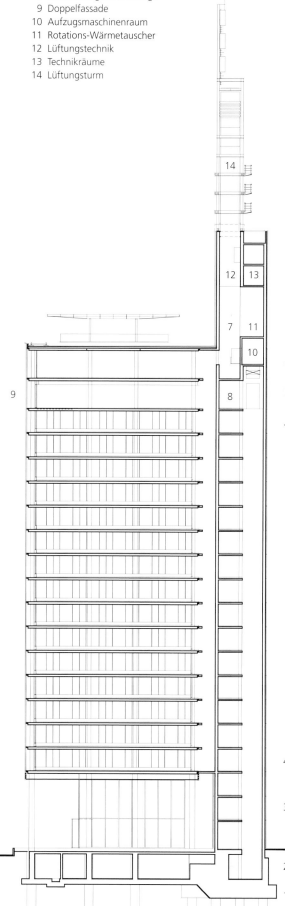

Section aa (for position see pp. 22 to 25)
scale 1:500

1 Foundations
2 Basement
3 Entrance hall
4 Office storeys
5 Hermes Lounge
6 Mechanical services storey
7 Air shaft
8 Access corridor; lifts
9 Two-layer facade
10 Lift machine room
11 Rotary fan heat-exchange unit
12 Ventilation technology
13 Mechanical services
14 Ventilation tower

Das täglich neue Wechselspiel in der Fassade
ist variantenreicher Ausdruck des Lebens
im Gebäudeinneren. Die ruhig wirkenden
seitlich stehenden Erschließungstürme
stabilisieren optisch die bauliche Gestalt

The subtle changes the facade
undergoes every day with the interplay of light
and shade are an expression of the life
within the building. The calm access towers
flanking the main volume visually stabilize the ensemble

Fassade direkt abgeführt. Die Fassade wirkt gleichzeitig als »Schutzschild«, um am Gebäude angreifende Winddrücke unterschiedlicher Intensität auszugleichen. Aus dem so gebildeten »Vorraum« werden die Büros über Schiebefenstertüren natürlich belüftet.

Das gewählte Lüftungskonzept sieht für jeden Arbeitsplatz ein zum Fassadenzwischenraum hin zu öffnendes raumhohes Schiebefenster vor. In jedem Arbeitsraum gibt es mindestens einen 1,80 m breiten Lüftungsflügel. Zusätzlich ist im Sockel ein kleiner Luftkanal in die Holzfensterkonstruktion integriert, dessen in den Fassadenmodulen eingebaute Auslässe die Lüftungsfunktion bei geschlossenem Fenster übernehmen. Über eine mechanische Verbindung werden sie bei geöffnetem Schiebefenster geschlossen, um Lüftungswärmeverluste über das offene Fenster zu vermeiden. Natürliche und mechanische Lüftung überlagern sich also. Der Nutzer kann die Menge und die Temperatur der Zuluft individuell bestimmen.

Die Abluft wird mit Hilfe eines zentralen Kanalsystems unter den Geschoßdecken in der Innenzone des Bürobereichs etagenweise gesammelt und über durchgehende vertikale Schächte als Fortluft an der oberen Gebäudespitze ins Freie geführt. Durch den thermischen Auftrieb wird die Luftbewegung im Gebäude unterstützt. So kommt durch Ausnutzen der großen Auftriebskräfte infolge der Höhe des Gebäudes und durch die am Gebäudekopf vorhandene hohe Windanströmung mit entsprechender Sogwirkung eine weitgehend durch Naturkräfte wirkende Lüftung zustande, deren ergänzender mechanischer Teil mit nur noch geringem Aufwand an Primärenergie betrieben wird. Im Kopf des Abluftschachts wird die Fortluft im Winter über einen Rotations-Wärmetauscher aus dem Gebäude geführt. Das Vorwärmen der Außenluft geschieht anhand dieses Wärmetauschers, der den Energieinhalt der Abluft bis zu 85 % zurückgewinnt.

storage elements for the heating and cooling systems laid in the screeds. In other words, the structural members themselves are subject to heating and cooling (also known as a "thermoactive slab" system). In conjunction with the ventilation installation, these thermal systems ensure an ideal indoor climate with scope for individual control. Internal heat sources (people, equipment, lamps, etc.) are more or less adequate to heat the building during the hours it is in use.

Unwanted heat, resulting from insolation in summer, is removed directly – without entering the offices – by the large volume of air flowing between the inner and outer facade layers. At the same time, the double-facade construction acts as a "protective shield", balancing out wind forces of varying intensity that hit the building. This buffer zone also forms a means of naturally ventilating the office spaces in conjunction with sliding windows.

As part of the ventilation concept, for each workplace a window is foreseen that opens on to the intermediate space in the facade. In every office, there is at least one 1.80-metre-wide, room-height sliding casement that can be opened for ventilation purposes. Depending on the size and position of the space, there can be more than one opening. In addition, a small air duct is incorporated in the apron panels of the timber casement construction. The outlets to these ducts, located in the facade modules, admit air when the windows are closed. In order to avoid heat losses through ventilation via open windows, the outlets are closed by a mechanical device when the sliding casements are opened. In this way, natural and mechanical forms of ventilation complement each other. Users can individually determine the amount and the temperature of the air supply according to personal requirements.

Exhaust air is collected storey by storey via a central system of conduits beneath the floor slabs in the inner zone of the office areas and drawn up through continuous vertical shafts to the top of the building, where it is emitted. Air circulation in the building is supported by thermal up-currents. In this way, a ventilation system was implemented that is activated largely by natural forces, exploiting the great uplift created by the height of the building and the strong winds at the top – which induce a powerful suction effect. The complementary mechanical installation operates with a minimum use of primary energy. In winter, vitiated air is drawn through a rotary heat-exchange unit at the top of the air-extract shaft before being discharged from the building. Up to 85 per cent of the energy content of the exhaust air is recovered in the process and is used to preheat the intake of external air.

Ansicht Süd, Maßstab 1:500
Ansicht West, Maßstab 1:500

 1 Bestehendes Verwaltungsgebäude
 2 Verbindungsgang zum Neubau
 3 Eingangshalle
 4 Zufahrt
 5 Doppelfassade Büroturm
 6 Möding Argeton Fassade
 7 Dachterrasse
 8 Plattform für Mobilfunkantennen
 9 Lüftungsturm
10 Lüftungselemente Doppelfassade
   zur natürlichen Lüftung
11 Flurfassade mit Lüftungsklappen
12 Treppenhaus Lamellenfenster

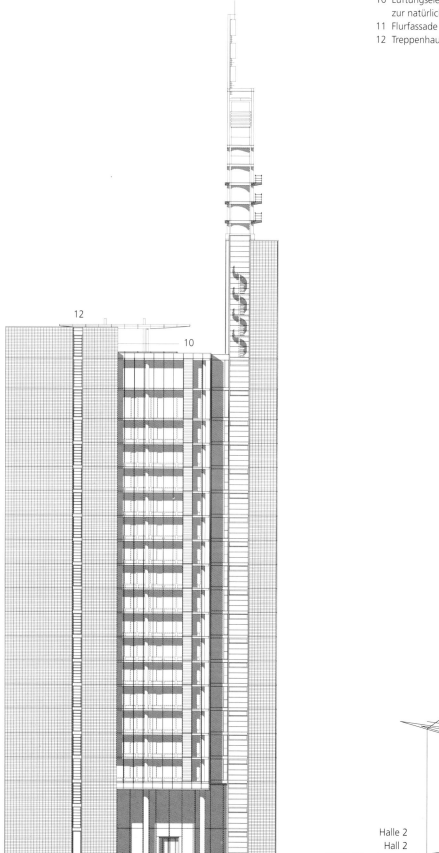

Eingangsbauwerk Nord
Northern entrance structure

Halle 2
Hall 2

1 Existing administration building
2 Link to new building
3 Entrance hall
4 Vehicle approach
5 Two-layer facade to office tower
6 Möding Argeton facade
7 Roof garden
8 Platform for cellular radio/telephone aerials
9 Ventilation tower
10 Elements in two-layer facade
   for natural ventilation
11 Corridor facade with ventilation louvres
12 Louvred windows in staircase

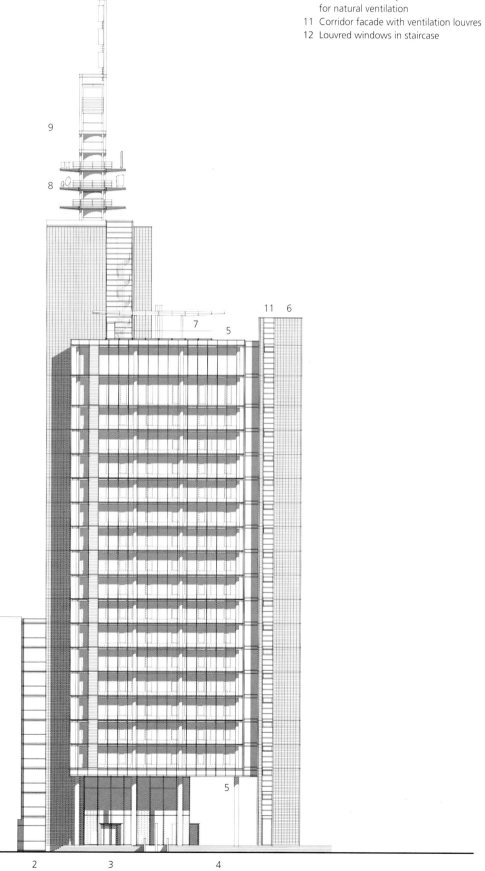

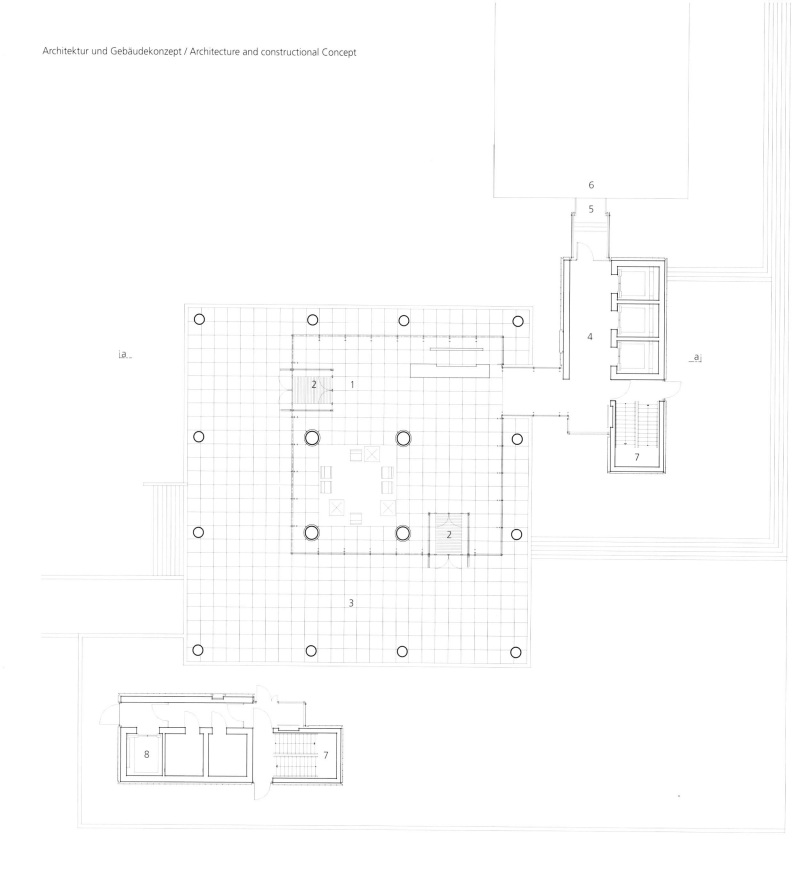

Grundriß Eingangshalle Erdgeschoß,
Maßstab 1:250

1 Eingangshalle
2 Windfänge
3 Zufahrt
4 Erschließungsflur, Aufzüge
5 Verbindungsgang
6 Bestehendes Verwaltungsgebäude
7 Sicherheitstreppenhaus
8 Feuerwehr- und Lastenaufzug

Ground floor plan with entrance hall
scale 1:250

1 Entrance hall
2 Wind lobbies
3 Vehicle access
4 Access corridor, Lifts
5 Link to existing administration building
6 Existing administration building
7 Escape staircase (with emergency exit)
8 Firefighting and goods lift

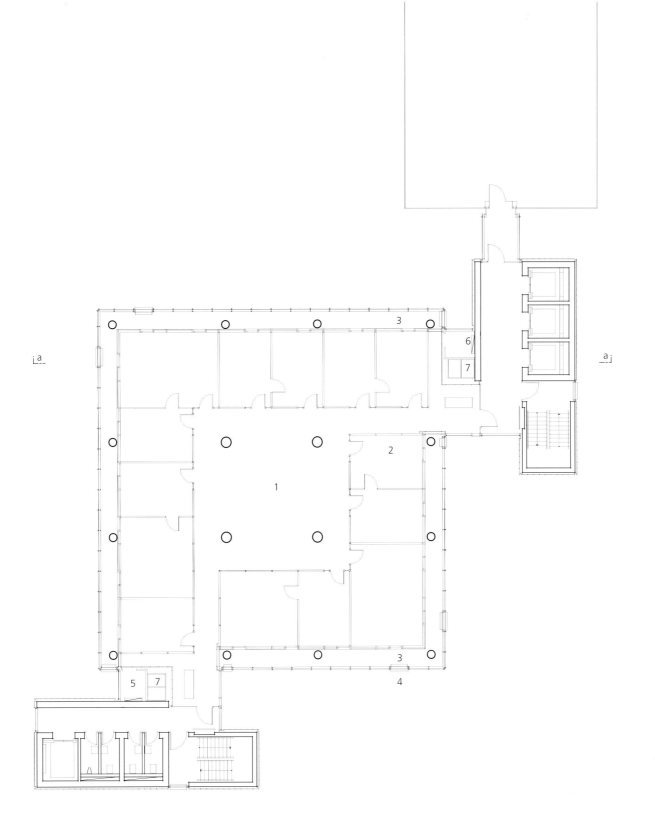

Grundriß Normalgeschoß,
variabel aufteilbar, Maßstab 1:250

Standard floor plan:
can be flexibly divided   scale 1:250

Erkennbar ist der Versatz des jeweils
auf die Gebäudemitte zentrierten Rasters der äußeren
und der inneren Fassaden

The grid axes of the inner and outer skins of
the two-layer facade are offset to each other.
Both grids are centred on the central axis of the
building.

1 Gemeinschaftszone
2 Büro
3 Zwischenraum Doppelfassade
4 Lüftungselemente
5 Unterverteilerraum
   Kommunikationstechnik
6 Unterverteilerraum
   Elektrotechnik
7 Zu- und Abluftschächte

1 Communal area
2 Office
3 Two-layer facades – intermediate space
4 Ventilation elements
5 Subdistribution room
   for communications technology
6 Subdistribution room
   for electrical installation
7 Air-supply and extract shafts

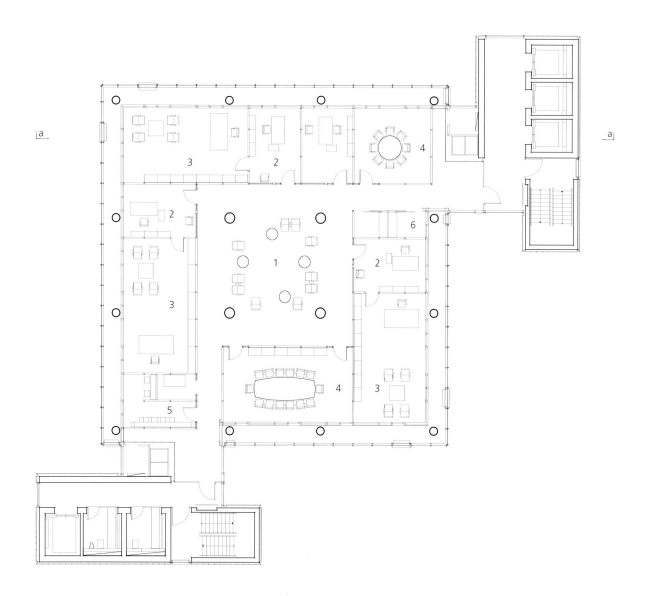

Grundriß Vorstandsgeschoß, Maßstab 1:250

Plan of executive floor with board rooms   scale 1:250

1 Besucher
2 Sekretariat
3 Büro
4 Besprechung
5 Teeküche
6 Garderobe

1 Visitors
2 Secretarial office
3 Office
4 Discussion
5 Kitchenette
6 Cloakroom

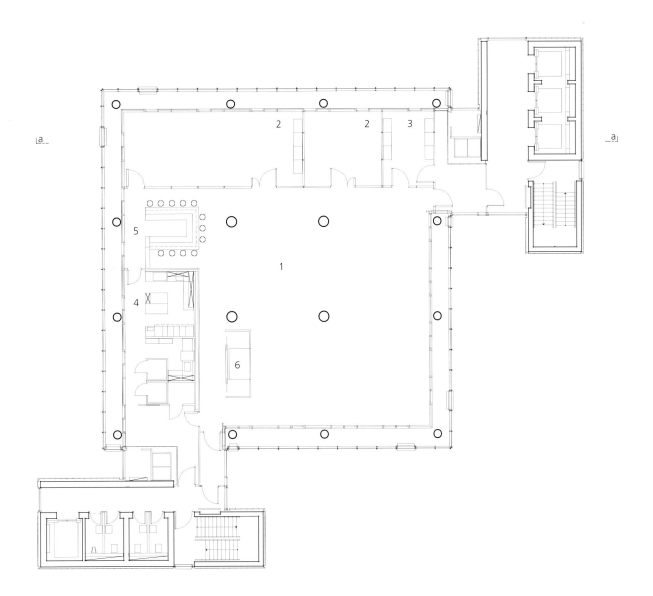

Grundriß »Hermes-Lounge«,
orientiert zum Grünraum, Maßstab 1:250

   1 Lounge
   2 Konferenz
   3 Garderobe
   4 Küche
   5 Bar
   6 Multimedia-Projektion

Plan of Hermes Lounge (18th floor)
oriented to landscaped external space   scale 1:250

   1 Lounge
   2 Conference rooms
   3 Cloakroom
   4 Kitchen
   5 Bar
   6 Multimedia projections

Blick über das Eingangsbauwerk Nord,
bei Tag und bei Nacht,
links das bestehende
neungeschossige Bürogebäude

View of tower over the northern entrance structure
during the day and at night;
the existing 9-storey office building
can be seen on the left

Isometrische Darstellung der technischen Systeme

Isometric Diagrams of Technical Systems

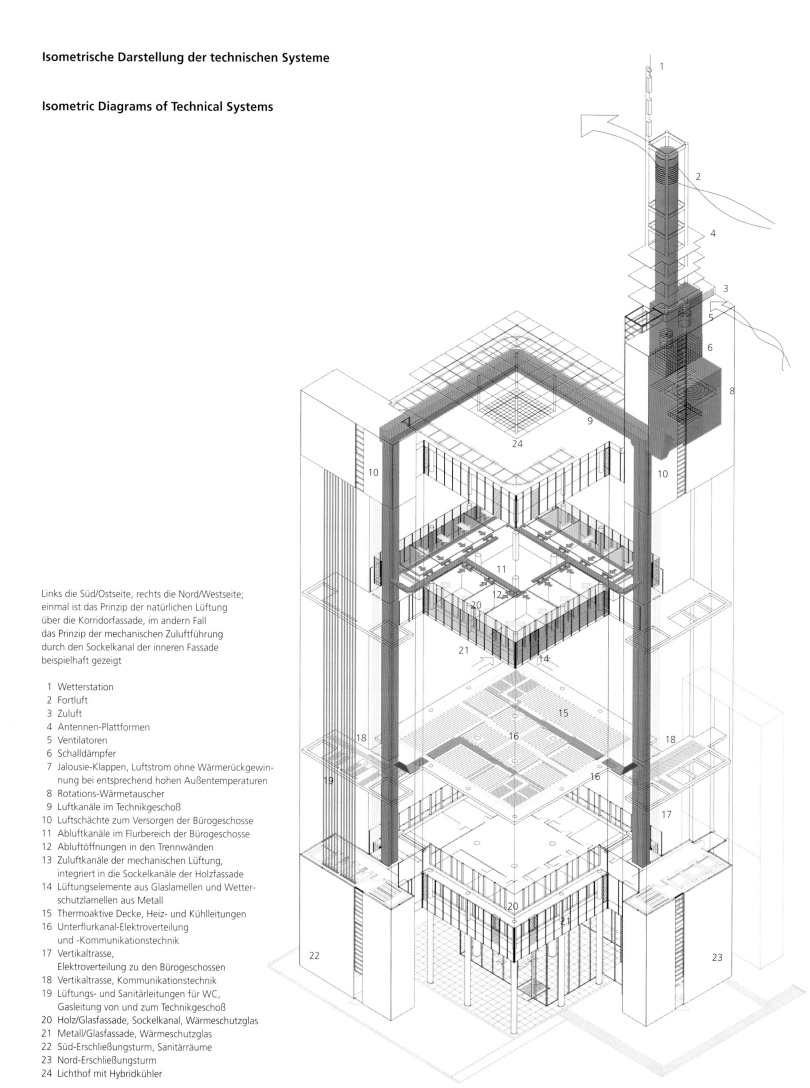

Links die Süd/Ostseite, rechts die Nord/Westseite;
einmal ist das Prinzip der natürlichen Lüftung
über die Korridorfassade, im andern Fall
das Prinzip der mechanischen Zuluftführung
durch den Sockelkanal der inneren Fassade
beispielhaft gezeigt

1 Wetterstation
2 Fortluft
3 Zuluft
4 Antennen-Plattformen
5 Ventilatoren
6 Schalldämpfer
7 Jalousie-Klappen, Luftstrom ohne Wärmerückgewin-
  nung bei entsprechend hohen Außentemperaturen
8 Rotations-Wärmetauscher
9 Luftkanäle im Technikgeschoß
10 Luftschächte zum Versorgen der Bürogeschosse
11 Abluftkanäle im Flurbereich der Bürogeschosse
12 Abluftöffnungen in den Trennwänden
13 Zuluftkanäle der mechanischen Lüftung,
   integriert in die Sockelkanäle der Holzfassade
14 Lüftungselemente aus Glaslamellen und Wetterschutzlamellen aus Metall
15 Thermoaktive Decke, Heiz- und Kühlleitungen
16 Unterflurkanal-Elektroverteilung
   und -Kommunikationstechnik
17 Vertikaltrasse,
   Elektroverteilung zu den Bürogeschossen
18 Vertikaltrasse, Kommunikationstechnik
19 Lüftungs- und Sanitärleitungen für WC,
   Gasleitung von und zum Technikgeschoß
20 Holz/Glasfassade, Sockelkanal, Wärmeschutzglas
21 Metall/Glasfassade, Wärmeschutzglas
22 Süd-Erschließungsturm, Sanitärräume
23 Nord-Erschließungsturm
24 Lichthof mit Hybridkühler

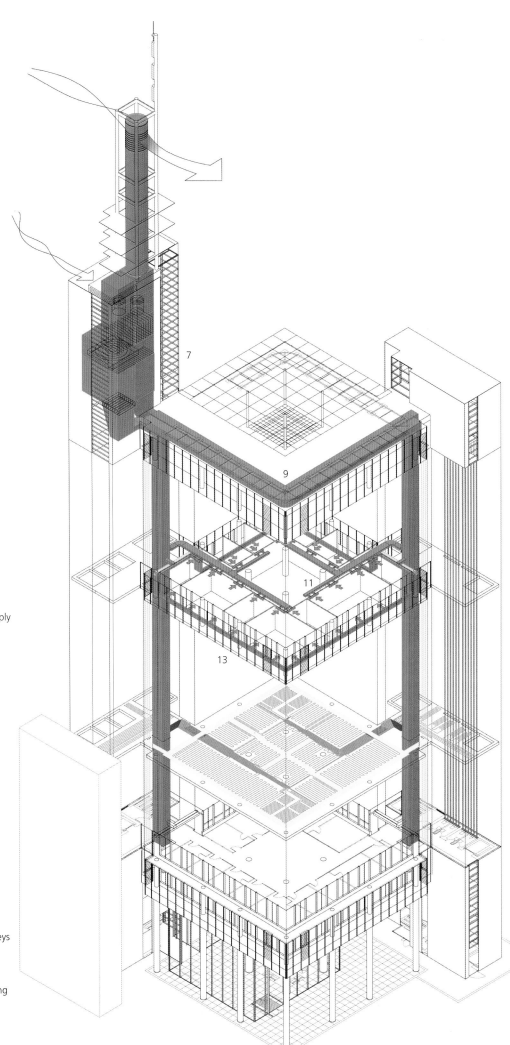

Left: the south and east faces; right, the north and west faces. In one case, the principle of natural ventilation via the corridor facade is shown; in the other case, the principle of mechanical air supply via ducts in the plinth zone of the inner facade

 1 Weather station
 2 Extract air
 3 Air supply
 4 Platform for aerials
 5 Fans
 6 Sound absorbers
 7 Louvre flaps; air stream without heat recovery
    when external temperatures sufficiently high
 8 Rotary heat-exchange unit
 9 Air ducts in mechanical services storey
10 Air-supply shafts to office storeys
11 Air-extract ducts in office storeys
12 Air-extract openings in internal partitions
13 Air-supply ducts for mechanical ventilation
    integrated in plinth ducts of wood facade
14 Ventilation elements, consisting of glass louvres
    and metal protective louvres
15 Heating and cooling runs for thermal activation
    of structural components
16 Subfloor conduit for electrical distribution and
    communications technology
17 Vertical runs: electrical distribution to office storeys
18 Vertical runs: communications technology
19 Ventilation and sanitary runs for WCs; gas runs
    to mechanical services storey
20 Wood and glass facade, plinth duct, low-E glazing
21 Metal and glass facade, low-E glazing
22 Southern access tower, sanitary facilities
23 Northern access tower
24 Light well with hybrid cooler

Gebäude-Aerodynamik und Raumklima

Dr. Richard A. Waters

1 Korrelation der Windgeschwindigkeit
und Richtungshäufigkeit

C_p-Werte der Hauptfassaden
für zwei beispielhafte Windrichtungen
2 Winddruck-Koeffizienten
Wind von Nordwesten
3 Winddruck-Koeffizienten
Wind von Südwesten

1 Correlation of wind velocity
and directional frequency

C_p value for main facades
for two sample wind directions
2 Wind-pressure coefficients:
north-west wind
3 Wind-pressure coefficients:
south-west wind

Beim Verwaltungsgebäude der Messe kommt eine doppelte Fassade zur Anwendung, die als Korridor das Gebäude einhüllt und eine Zwischentemperaturzone als Pufferbereich bildet. Dieser »Puffer« hat auf das Gebäudeklima folgende Auswirkungen:

• Es entsteht eine Zone rund um die Büros, in der die Auswirkungen des Windeinflusses – speziell in größerer Höhe – gemindert werden.

• Die Nutzer der Büros können auf ihr Arbeitsumfeld selbst Einfluß nehmen und sind in der Lage, Fenster auch in größerer Höhe zu öffnen.

• Die Strategie natürlicher Lüftung ergänzt und unterstützt das mechanische Heiz- und Kühlsystem in den Büroetagen.

• Der »Pufferbereich« bietet dem Architekten Vorteile für die Gestaltung des Tragwerks, den Brandschutz und für die Konstruktion.

Ein Kanal mit 300 mm Durchmesser verbindet den Süd-Ost- mit dem Nord-West-Bereich. Jeder »Pufferbereich« ist geschoßhoch – so entsteht ein horizontaler Luftkanal auf allen Seiten des Gebäudes. Seine Ober- und Unterseite formen die umlaufenden Deckenplatten, die 1 m breit zwischen den beiden Fassadenebenen liegen, welche ihrerseits die Seiten des Kanals bilden. Dies bedeutet, daß so jedes Geschoß einen eigenen Brandabschnitt bildet.

Acht 3 m hohe Streifen mit Lüftungslamellen liegen in der äußeren Fassadenebene, um den Luftein- und -austritt in den Luftkorridor zu ermöglichen. Die Lamellen können in 6 unterschiedliche Positionen eingestellt werden, was 720 unterschiedliche Varianten pro Etage ermöglicht bzw. rund 14.000 für das gesamte Gebäude. Die Einstellungen der Lamellenöffnungen erfolgen durch gespeicherte Echtzeitvorgaben, wobei Daten von Wetterstationen, Windkanal-Werte und Rechenwerte Eingang finden.

6 Temperaturmeßpunkte sind eingerichtet, um die minimale, maximale und die errechnete Durchschnittstemperatur im Luftkorridor zu steuern.

Unterschiedliche Lüftungsstrategien werden eingesetzt für:

• Die unterschiedlichen Jahreszeiten. Sie wurden definiert für den Bereich der jeweiligen Außenlufttemperatur, nicht jedoch über das Datum. Nicht Tag und Uhrzeit sind nämlich hier von Bedeutung, sondern diese Temperatur, die das Raumklima im Pufferbereich beeinflußt. Grob gesprochen, stimmen die ausgewählten Temperaturbereiche in etwa überein mit: Frühjahr / Sommer / Hochsommer / Herbst / Winter / tiefer Winter.

• Die wechselnde Tageszeit.

• Das Maß des solaren Energieeintrags.

• Die externe Windgeschwindigkeit und Windrichtung.

Ein maßstäbliches Modell des Hochhauses wurde im Windkanal untersucht. Die Druckverhältnisse wurden an einigen hundert Stellen und für viele unterschiedliche Windrichtungen gemessen.

Die Diagramme zeigen Kurven, in denen die Druckbeiwerte (C_p) gleicher Höhe für die Hauptfassaden bezogen auf zwei ausgewählte Windrichtungen angegeben sind.

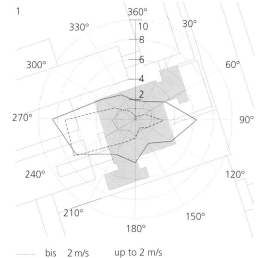

.... bis 2 m/s	up to 2 m/s
- - - - 2 bis 5 m/s	2 to 5 m/s
——— über 5 m/s	more than 5 m/s

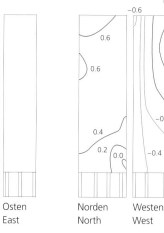

Süden / Osten   Norden / Westen
South / East   North / West

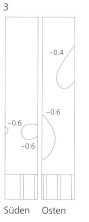

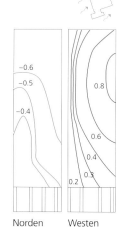

Süden Osten   Norden Westen

Schema der natürlichen Luftführung,
von außen nach innen
Vertikalschnitt (Übergangszeit), Maßstab 1:500

Diagram of natural airflow
from outside to inside
Vertical section (transitional period) scale 1:500

NEW YORK INSTITUTE
OF TECHNOLOGY LIBRARY

≫	Zuluft		Air supply
≫	Abluft		Air extract
▬	Abluftschacht mit Kaminwirkung		Air-extract shaft with "stack" effect

Aerodynamics and Internal Climate of Building

Dr Richard A. Waters

Schema der natürlichen Luftführung, von außen nach innen (Horizontalschnitte)

1 Doppelfassade (Korridorfassade) Winter
2 Doppelfassade (Korridorfassade) Übergangszeit
3 Doppelfassade (Korridorfassade) Hochsommer

+...+++   Winddruck
-...---   Windsog
——○   Fassadenöffnung
●   Temperaturfühler
→   Außenluft, Fortluft
▶▶▶   Fassadenstrom
≥ ≫   Zuluft, Abluft
⬚⬚⬚   Bypass
◼━▭   Abluftschacht

Diagram of natural airflow, from outside to inside (horizontal sections)

1 Two-layer facade (corridor facade) winter
2 Two-layer facade (corridor facade) transitional period
3 Two-layer facade (corridor facade) high summer

+...+++   Wind pressure
-...---   Wind suction
——○   Facade opening
●   Temperature sensor
→   External air, exhaust air
▶▶▶   Airflow through corridor facade
≥ ≫   Air supply, air extract
⬚⬚⬚   Bypass
◼━▭   Air-extract shaft

The DMAG Tower has a two-layer facade that forms an environmental buffer around the building.

This buffer provides the opportunity for environmental control in various ways.

- It forms a zone around the offices in which the effects of winds at high level can be reduced.
- Office users can control their working environment and open windows at high level.
- The natural ventilation strategy supplements and supports the mechanical heating and cooling system used in the offices.
- In addition, the buffer zone provides the architects with structural, fire-engineering and constructional advantages.

A 300 mm diameter duct links the buffer zones to the north and west with those to the south and east. The intermediate space between the facade layers is divided into storey-height segments, thereby creating a series of horizontal air ducts around the building. The top and bottom of the buffer spaces are formed by the concrete floor slabs, which cantilever out one metre beyond the office facades. This means that each floor of the building represents a self-contained fire zone.

In the outer skin of the facade are eight 3-metre-high strips with ventilation louvres that allow the passage of air into and out of the intermediate corridors. The louvres can be set in six different positions, which allow 720 permutations per storey or some 14,000 for the entire building. The adjustment of the louvres is controlled by real-time computerized input, using system data. This includes information from weather stations, wind-tunnel tests and analytical values. Six temperature measurement points were installed to control the minimum, maximum and estimated mean temperature values in the intermediate corridor.

Different opening strategies are applied for the following situations.

- The different seasons of the year. In this case, the strategy was determined according to relevant external temperatures and not according to the date. This strategy was adopted because it is the external temperature – and not the date and time of day – that is of importance to the environmental conditions within the buffer zone. In broad terms, the temperature ranges selected correspond to spring, summer, high summer, autumn, winter and deep winter.
- The time of day.
- The amount of solar energy impacting the facades.
- The external wind speed and direction.

A scale model of the tower was tested in a wind tunnel.

Pressure conditions were measured at several hundred locations and for many different wind directions.

The illustrations show contours indicating where the pressure coefficient (C_p) is identical on the main facades in relation to two sample wind directions.

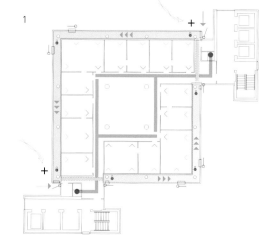

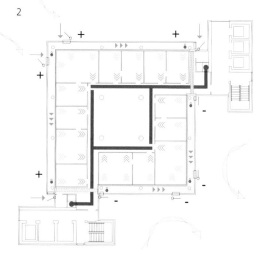

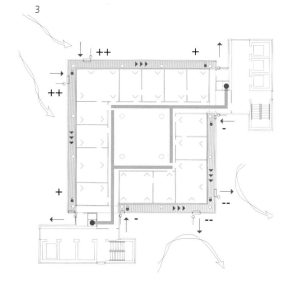

Klima-Vertikalschnitt durch ein Bürogeschoß

Vertical section through office storey

1 Winter
2 Sommer

1 Winter
2 Summer

1
Thermoaktive Decke / Thermoactive floor slab

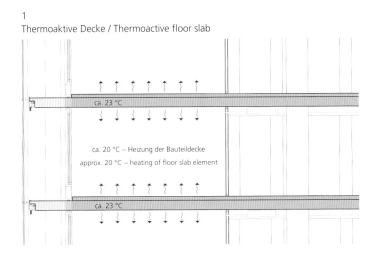

ca. 23 °C

ca. 20 °C – Heizung der Bauteildecke
approx. 20 °C – heating of floor slab element

ca. 23 °C

1
Lüftung / Ventilation

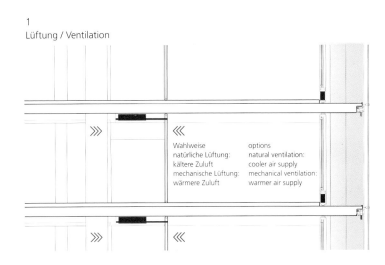

Wahlweise	options
natürliche Lüftung:	natural ventilation:
kältere Zuluft	cooler air supply
mechanische Lüftung:	mechanical ventilation:
wärmere Zuluft	warmer air supply

2
Thermoaktive Decke / Thermoactive floor slab

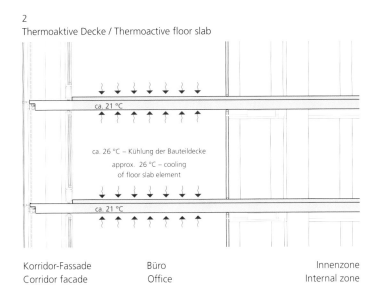

ca. 21 °C

ca. 26 °C – Kühlung der Bauteildecke
approx. 26 °C – cooling
of floor slab element

ca. 21 °C

2
Lüftung / Ventilation

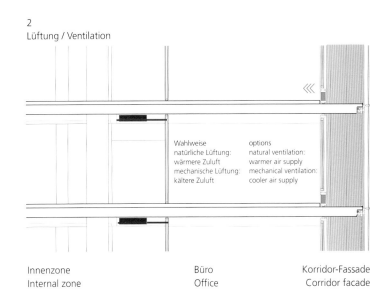

Wahlweise	options
natürliche Lüftung:	natural ventilation:
wärmere Zuluft	warmer air supply
mechanische Lüftung:	mechanical ventilation:
kältere Zuluft	cooler air supply

Korridor-Fassade
Corridor facade

Büro
Office

Innenzone
Internal zone

Innenzone
Internal zone

Büro
Office

Korridor-Fassade
Corridor facade

Die Doppelfassade innen:
Holz und Glas

Inner Skin of Two-Layer Facade:
Wood and Glass

1 Sockel mit Lüftungselement,
  darüber Schiebe-Fenstertür
2 Lüftungskanäle in den
  vorgefertigten Fassadenbauteilen
3 Montage der Innenfassade
4 Blick von außen durch die Metall/Glasfassade
  auf die innere, witterungsgeschützte Holzfassade
5 Geöffnete Schiebe-Fenstertür
6 Geöffnetes Lüftungselement vom Korridor aus
7 Blick in den Zwischentemperaturbereich
  der Doppelfassade; die hier liegenden Außenstützen
  ermöglichen stützenfreie Büroräume
  (siehe Grundrisse Seite 22 bis 25)

4

5

1

6

2

3

1 Apron wall with ventilation element beneath sliding
  casement
2 Ventilation ducts in prefabricated facade elements
3 Assembly of internal facade
4 View from outside through metal and glass facade
  to inner wood and glass facade protected against
  the weather
5 Sliding French window in open position
6 Open ventilation element in corridor
7 View along intermediate temperature zone between
  two skins of double facade. By locating the columns
  in the corridor, the offices remain column-free
  (see plans pp. 22 to 25)

Die Doppelfassade außen:
Metall und Glas

Outer Skin of Two-Layer Facade:
Metal and Glass

1 Montage der Lüftungslamellen
2 Blick von innen auf die Glaslamellen
3 Blick auf eine Sprosse der filigranen Metall/
  Glasfassade. Das eigens entwickelte Aluminium-
  Abdeckprofil dient auch als Führungsschiene für die
  Fassadenreinigungsanlage
4 Blick von oben auf den Montagewagen der Fassade
5 Zur Montage bereitliegende Vertikalsprossen
6 und 7 Eckausbildung

1 Assembly of ventilation louvres

2 Internal view of glass louvres

3 Window division: part of slenderly dimensioned metal and glass facade construction. The specially developed aluminium cover strip also serves as a guide track for the facade cleaning equipment

4 View of facade assembly cradle from above

5 Window mullions awaiting assembly

6 and 7 Corner detail of building

6

7

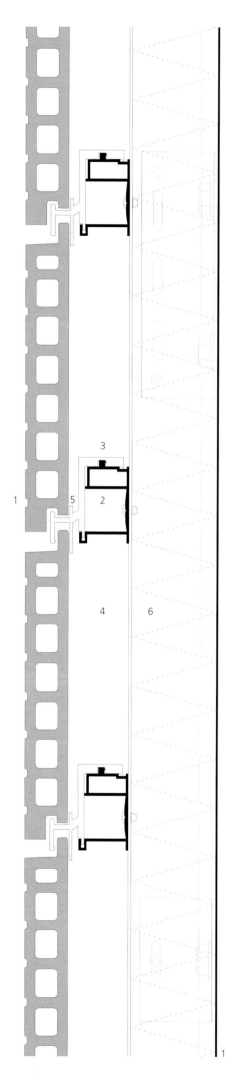

Die Ziegelfassade an den Erschließungstürmen

Clay-Tile Facade to Access Towers

1 Vertikalschnitt Möding Argeton Fassade (DBP)

  1 Argeton Ziegelplatte, 30 mm stark, mit Querrillen
  2 Alu-Klipsprofil
  3 Alu-Klipshalter
  4 Lüftungsspalt
  5 Kapillare Trennung
  6 Wärmedämmung zwischen
    vertikalen Grundprofilen

2 und 4 Musterfassade mit Farbversuch:
  Helles Perlgrau als neue Einzelplatte
3 Montagezustand mit Alu-Tragprofilen
5 Ziegelfassade mit Lüftungsfensterband
6 Außenliegende Erschließungstürme,
  mit Ziegelfassade bekleidet, Ostansicht

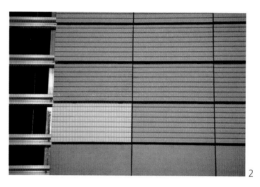

1 Vertical section through Möding Argeton facade
  (patended)

  1 30 mm Argeton clay tiles with horizontal grooves
  2 aluminium bearer
  3 aluminium fixing clip
  4 cavity
  5 anti-capillary gap
  6 thermal insulation between vertical fixing elements

2 and 4 Sample facade panels for colour trials:
  new facing tiles in pale pearl-grey
3 Facade assembly with aluminium bearers
5 Clay-tile facade with ventilating window strip
6 View from east with main tower flanked
  by access towers: clay-tile facade cladding

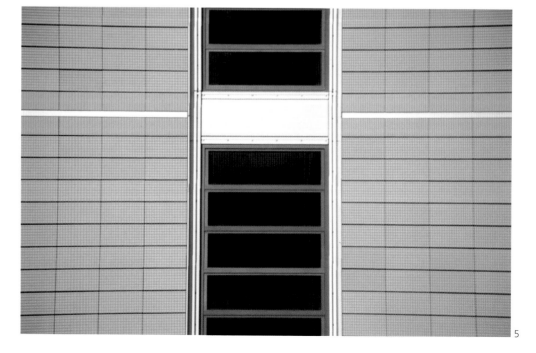

Das Tragwerk

Dr.-Ing. Erhard Garske

Load-Bearing Structure

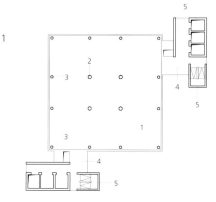

1

Überblick

Bei Hochhäusern dominieren nicht selten Überlegungen zum Abtragen der Wind- und Aussteifungslasten das Gebäudekonzept grundsätzlich. Für das Verwaltungsgebäude – ein eher niedriges Hochhaus – waren diese Einwirkungen zwar noch nicht konzeptionell bestimmend, jedoch richteten sich die Abmessungen wesentlicher Bauteile nach Beanspruchungen aus diesen Einwirkungen.

Die prinzipielle Lastabtragung ist bei diesem Gebäude sehr klar und anschaulich. Die vertikalen Einwirkungen in den Geschossen werden im Bürotrakt über 30 cm dicke Flachdecken aus Stahlbeton auf 16 Rundstützen übertragen (Bild 1), die über alle oberirdischen Vollgeschosse durchgehen und ihre Lasten auf die trägerrostartig angeordneten Wände des Untergeschosses übertragen (Bild 2). In den Bereichen der aussteifenden Gebäudekerne im Nordosten und Südwesten übernehmen diese Aufgaben 20 cm dicke Stahlbetondecken und die Stahlbetonwände der Kerne. Diese Gebäudekerne schließen biegesteif an das massive Untergeschoß an, das mit seiner Decke, den trägerrostartig angeordneten Wänden und der Bodenplatte einen insgesamt sehr steifen, kastenartigen Gründungskörper bildet (Bild 3). Baubegleitende Messungen zeigten, daß sich das angestrebte, sehr gleichmäßige Setzungsverhalten des Gebäudes auch real einstellt. Das eigentliche Übertragen der Gebäudelasten in den Baugrund geschieht mit einer Kombination aus Flach- und Pfahlgründung.

Zum Aufnehmen und sicheren Abtragen der Wind- und Aussteifungslasten – letztere entstehen beispielsweise durch unplanmäßige Stützenschiefstellungen – bilden die Erschließungstürme im Nordosten und Südwesten zusammen mit den Geschoßdecken ein stabiles Tragsystem. Hierbei wirken die Geschoßdecken als Scheiben, d.h. sie werden in ihrer Ebene beansprucht und übertragen die horizontalen Einwirkungen in die Kernwände. Sie erzwingen auch ein Mitwirken der einzelnen Kernteile am Abtragen der Lasten in dem Maß, wie es ihrer

Introduction

The basic concept of many high-rise buildings is dominated by considerations such as the transmission of wind and bracing loads. Although these factors did not determine the concept for the new administration building – a relatively low tower block – the dimensions of important sections of the building do reflect the loading from these sources.

The main load-bearing system of the building is clearly defined and comprehensible. Within the various storeys of the office tract, loads are transmitted vertically downwards via 30-centimetre reinforced concrete flat slabs supported by 16 round columns (ill. 1). The columns extend through all full storeys above ground level and transmit their loads to the basement walls, which are laid out in a form resembling a grid of beams (ill. 2). In the areas of the stiffening cores to the north-east and south-west, this function is performed by 20-centimetre reinforced concrete floor slabs and the reinforced concrete walls of the cores. The cores are rigidly connected to the solid basement structure – an extremely stiff, box-like foundation construction, comprising the ground floor slab, the grid-like layout of the walls and the base slab (ill. 3). Measurements made during the construction process showed that the even settlement expected of this type of structure actually took place. The transmission of loads from the building to the ground occurs via a combination of flat slab foundations and piles.

The core structures to the north-east and south-west of the main tower, in combination with the floor slabs, form a stable load-bearing system capable of absorbing wind and bracing loads and transmitting them safely to the ground. Bracing loads may be caused, for example, by unintentional non-verticality in certain columns. In this respect, the floor slabs function as rigid membranes; in other words, they bear and transmit horizontal loads in their plane to the core walls. They also ensure that individual elements of the core structures participate in the trans-

1 Tragende Bauteile im Regelgeschoß
  Maßstab 1:750

  1 Stahlbetonflachdecke d=30 cm, B 45
  2 Mittelstützen d=70 cm, B 45 / B 95
  3 Rand- und Eckstützen d=50 cm, B 45 / B 95
  4 Stahlbetondecke im Bereich der Kerne, B 45
  5 Stahlbetonwände der Kerne
    d=30 bzw. 40 cm, B 45

1 Structural elements on standard floors
  scale 1:750

  1 30 cm reinforced concrete flat slab (B 45)
  2 70 cm dia. middle columns (B 45/B 95)
  3 50 cm dia. edge and corner columns (B 45/B 95)
  4 reinforced concrete floor slab in core towers (B 45)
  5 30 and 40 cm reinforced concrete walls
    to core towers (B 45)

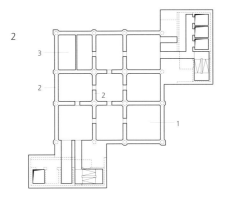

3 Tragendes Stahlbetonskelett mit kastenartig
   ausgebildetem Untergeschoß Maßstab 1:750

   1 Flachdecken d=30 cm, B 45
   2 Mittelstützen d=70 cm / d=90 cm, B 45 / B 95
   3 Rand- und Eckstützen d=70 cm / d=50 cm,
     B 45 / B 95
   4 Stahlbetondecke im Bereich der Kerne
     d=20 cm, B 45
   5 Stahlbetonwände der Kerne
     d=30 cm bzw. d=40 cm, B 45
   6 Untergeschoß – ausgebildet als kastenartiger
     Gründungskörper

3 Load-bearing reinforced concrete skeleton frame with
   beam-grid box-form basement structure scale 1:750

   1 30 cm flat slabs (B 45)
   2 70 and 90 cm dia. middle columns (B 45/B 95)
   3 70 and 50 cm dia. edge and corner columns
     (B 45/B 95)
   4 20 cm reinforced concrete floor slab
     in cores (B 45)
   5 30 and 40 cm reinforced concrete walls
     to cores (B 45)
   6 basement – constructed as box-like grid foundation
     volume

2 Tragende Bauteile im Untergeschoß
   Maßstab 1:750

   1 Stahlbetondecke d=30 cm, B 35
   2 Trägerrostartig angeordnete Stahlbetonwände
     d=75 cm, B 35
   3 Stahlbetonplatte d=75 cm, B 35

2 Structural elements in basement
   scale 1:750

   1 30 cm reinforced concrete floor slab (B 35)
   2 75 cm reinforced concrete walls in
     beam-grid layout (B 35)
   3 75 cm reinforced concrete slab (B 35)

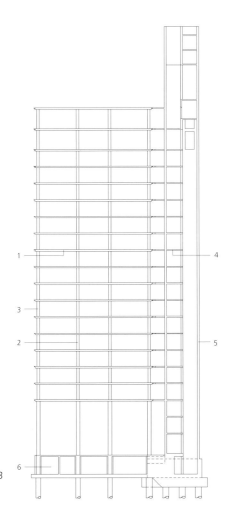

jeweiligen Steifigkeit entspricht. Das mögliche rahmenartige Tragverhalten der Stützen und Geschoßdecken wird bei dieser baumechanischen Modellbildung zunächst außer acht gelassen. Die Erschließungstürme im Nordosten und Südwesten bestehen aus einem kastenartigen Querschnitt (Fahrstuhlschächte), einem U–förmigen Querschnittsteil (Treppenhäuser) und einer einzelnen Stahlbetonwand (Bild 2). Statisch wirken die Erschließungstürme wie Kragarme, die im kastenartig ausgebildeten Gründungskörper des Untergeschosses eingespannt sind.

Besonderheiten
Das Tragwerk des neuen Verwaltungsgebäudes ist durch einige Besonderheiten gekennzeichnet. Sie ergaben sich einerseits aus wirtschaftlichen Überlegungen und andererseits aus dem architektonischen Konzept.

Im allgemeinen werden Abmessungen tragender Bauteile nach baumechanischen Erfordernissen festgelegt. Dabei sind zwei ganz wesentliche Bedingungen zu beachten bzw. nachzuweisen: Einerseits muß die Beanspruchung, die ein Bauteil versagen läßt, einen genügend großen Sicherheitsabstand von den real auftretenden Beanspruchungen haben, d.h. das Bauteil muß ausreichend tragfähig sein. Andererseits sind die Abmessungen der Bauteile so festzulegen, daß diese ausreichend gebrauchstauglich und dauerhaft sind. Im Stahlbetonbau sollen durch Einhalten bestimmter Regeln hauptsächlich zu große Verformungen und zu breite Risse vermieden werden. Bei üblichen Hochbauten reichen diese statischen Untersuchungen meist aus, um die notwendige Tragfähigkeit und Gebrauchstauglichkeit zu gewährleisten. Die Entwicklung von Baustoffen immer höherer Festigkeiten und die damit einhergehende Planung und Ausführung immer schlankerer Bauteile erfordert in zunehmendem Maße auch die dynamische Analyse bestimmter Bauteile. Dies wurde auch beim neuen Verwaltungsgebäude deutlich.

mission of loads – to a degree corresponding to the rigidity of each part. The potential frame-like load-bearing behaviour of the columns and floor slabs was initially ignored in creating this model of the structural mechanics. The core structures to the northeast and south-west consist of box-like cross-sections (lift shafts), an element with a U-shaped cross-section (staircase), and a single reinforced concrete wall (ill. 2). Structurally, the cores function rather like cantilevered arms rigidly fixed to the box-like foundation structure of the basement.

Special aspects
The load-bearing structure of the new administration building exhibits a number of special features that will be described below. They were the outcome of two sets of constraints: economic considerations on the one hand, and the architectural concept on the other.

In general, the dimensions of load-bearing members are determined according to the laws of structural mechanics. Two fundamental aspects have to be observed or proved in this context. First, the loading that would cause a structural member to collapse has to be removed by a sufficient safety margin from the actual loading that will occur. In other words, the member has to have an adequate load-bearing capacity. Second, the dimensions of the structural elements have to be determined in such a way that the members are robust, durable and suitable for practical use. In reinforced concrete construction, certain rules are observed principally to avoid excessive deformation and overwide cracking. In most conventional high-rise buildings, structural studies of this kind are adequate to guarantee the required load-bearing capacity and practical efficiency. The development of building materials of ever greater strength, however – and the planning and construction of components with increasingly slender dimensions to which this leads – necessitates a dynamic analysis of certain structural elements. This became clear

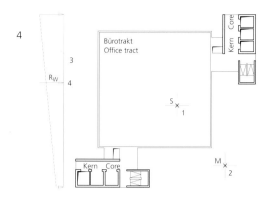

Beispielsweise sah der Sondervorschlag einer Baufirma die Ausführung von nur 22 cm dicken, vorgespannten Geschoßdecken vor. Eine Schwingungsuntersuchung zeigte jedoch, daß eine Anregung dieser Decken bereits durch gehende Personen wahrscheinlich ist. Der Sondervorschlag wurde daher ausgeschieden.

Gebäudeaussteifung

Hochhäuser bzw. ihre Aussteifungssysteme sind typische Beispiele für die Notwendigkeit von baudynamischen Untersuchungen. Bereits die Windbelastung hängt bei schlanken Konstruktionen nicht mehr nur von der Windgeschwindigkeit und der äußeren Gebäudeform ab, sondern auch vom dynamischen Verhalten der Konstruktion selbst. Zum Ermitteln der für dieses Bauwerk anzusetzenden statischen Ersatzwindlast mußte auch die kleinste Eigenfrequenz des Aussteifungssystems bestimmt werden, woraus unter Hinzunahme weiterer Parameter der sogenannte Böenreaktionsfaktor errechnet werden kann. Die statische Ersatzwindlast ist dann, vereinfacht gesagt, die mit dem Böenreaktionsfaktor erhöhte »normale Windlast«.

Das Aufnehmen und das sichere Abtragen dieser Windeinwirkungen war im vorliegenden Fall eine zentrale Aufgabe des Tragwerksplaners. Anordnung und Ausbildung der aussteifenden Bauteile widersprachen im Grundsatz baumechanischen Idealvorstellungen zum Aussteifen von Hochhäusern. Zum einen erhalten die außenliegenden Erschließungstürme nur wenig Auflast aus den Geschoßdecken, zum anderen sind Gebäudeschwerpunkt (S) – damit auch die resultierende Windkraft – und der Drehruhepunkt (M) aller Aussteifungsquerschnitte ziemlich weit voneinander entfernt (Bild 4). Die angreifenden Windlasten verbiegen somit nicht nur das aussteifende System, sondern sie erzeugen auch eine Verdrehung des Systems um die vertikale Achse durch den Drehruhepunkt. Ferner sind die Querschnitte der aussteifenden Gebäudekerne

in the planning of the new administration building.

For example, a construction firm made a special proposal to execute prestressed floor slabs to a thickness of only 22 centimetres. An investigation of vibration behaviour, however, showed that the proposed slabs would probably be activated merely by pedestrian traffic. The special proposal was, therefore, rejected.

Bracing the building

High-rise blocks, or their bracing systems, are typical examples of structures where the constructional dynamics have to be investigated. For example, with slender forms of construction, the wind loading will depend not only on the wind speed and the external form of the building, but on the dynamic behaviour of the structure itself. In calculating the relevant equivalent wind load for the present building, it was necessary to determine the minimum resonance frequency of the bracing system. From this and other parameters, it was possible to calculate the so-called gust-reaction factor. The structural equivalent wind load is then, expressed in simple terms, the "normal wind load" augmented by the gust-reaction factor.

In the present project, the absorption and safe transmission of these wind loads was of central importance for the structural engineers. In terms of structural mechanics, the layout and design of the bracing elements were, in principle, contrary to ideal concepts of bracing high-rise buildings. On the one hand, the cores receive only a small amount of the live loads from the floor slabs. On the other hand, the centre of gravity of the building (S) – and thus the resultant wind loads – and the torsional shear centre (M) of the cross-sections of all bracing members are fairly far apart (ill. 4). Wind loads not only subject the bracing system to bending; they also result in a pivoting of the system about its vertical axis through the torsional shear centre. Furthermore, because of the position

Vertikalschnitt
Vertical section

Untersicht
View from below

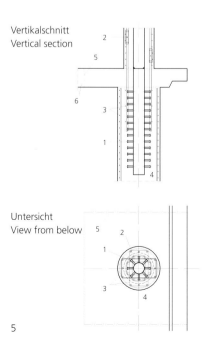

bei ungünstiger Windbeanspruchung nicht mehr voll überdrückt. Dies ist eine Folge der Anordnung der außenliegenden Erschließungstürme und der damit verbundenen geringen Auflast aus den Geschoßdecken. Es kann daher rechnerisch zum Auftreten horizontaler Risse in den aussteifenden Bauteilen kommen, die zwar typisch für das Tragverhalten biegebeanspruchter Stahlbetonbauteile sind, jedoch eine Abnahme der Steifigkeit zur Folge haben.

Da die gewählte Anordnung der Erschließungstürme jedoch andere, bereits zuvor beschriebene, wesentliche Vorteile bot, wurde sie dennoch verwirklicht.

Es erwies sich für die Nachweise der Tragfähigkeit als zweckmäßig, ausschließlich die Erschließungstürme als statisch wirksam anzusetzen und bei Nachweisen der Gebrauchstauglichkeit auch die Rahmentragwirkung der Decken und Rundstützen zu nutzen. Zur Gebrauchstauglichkeit waren über sonst übliche statische Berechnungen hinausgehende Nachweise zu führen, die auch die in den oberen Geschossen unter Windeinwirkung zu erwartenden Beschleunigungen erfassen (baudynamische Untersuchung). Damit war sichergestellt, daß diese windinduzierten Beschleunigungen des Gebäudes von Personen nicht als unangenehm empfunden werden. Zum Ermitteln von Verformungen der aussteifenden Stahlbetonbauteile wurden allgemein anerkannte Materialgesetze für das mechanische Verhalten des – auch gerissenen – Stahlbetons genutzt, die allerdings in der zur Planungsphase gültigen Fassung der deutschen Stahlbetonnorm noch nicht enthalten waren.

Stützen aus hochfestem Beton

Eine weitere Besonderheit des Gebäudes stellen die Rundstützen aus hochfestem Beton (B 95) in den unteren 12 Geschossen dar. Dieser neuartige Beton ermöglichte es, den Querschnitt der Stützen zu minimieren und über die gesamte Gebäudehöhe gleich auszuführen. Vorteile ergaben sich daraus natür-

of the external cores and the low degree of loading on the floor slabs, unfavourable wind loads may result in the cross-sections of the bracing core structures no longer being subject to excessive wind loading. Calculations reveal a potential horizontal cracking of the bracing elements. Although this is typical of the load-bearing behaviour of reinforced concrete elements subject to bending loads, it results in reduced rigidity.

Since the layout of the core structures offered other major advantages, however, as described above, the building was realized in this form. In providing proof of the load-bearing capacity, it was practical to regard only the core tracts as structurally effective. In providing proof of functional efficiency, the framing action of the floor slabs and round columns was also taken into account. In calculating the functional efficiency, additional proof had to be provided over and above the usual structural calculations. The anticipated wind-excited motion on the upper floors (investigation of constructional dynamics) had to be taken into account as well. This served to demonstrate that the wind-excited motion of the building was not perceived as an unpleasant phenomenon by people within. In determining the degree of deformation in the reinforced concrete bracing elements, generally recognized laws of materials were used for the mechanical behaviour of reinforced concrete (even in a cracked state). These were not contained in the version of the German reinforced concrete standards in force during the planning stage, however.

Columns in high-strength concrete

The round columns in the lower 12 storeys, executed in high-strength concrete (B 95), are yet another special feature of the building. This new type of concrete allowed the cross-sectional area of the columns to be minimized and the same cross-section to be maintained over the full height of the building. This has advantages during the finishings

6

7 Gebäudegründung Maßstab 1:750

1 Trägerrostartige Wände im Untergeschoß
2 Bodenplatte d=75 cm, B 35
3 Massive Fundamentkörper unter den Kernen
4 Bohrpfähle Ø 90 cm
5 Bohrpfähle Ø 120 cm

7 Foundation plan scale 1:750

1 Box-like beam grid of walls in basement
2 75 cm ground slab (B 35)
3 Solid foundation volume beneath cores
4 90 cm dia. bored piles
5 120 cm dia. bored piles

lich für den Ausbau. Die Stützen konnten so an die von oben nach unten stark zunehmende Beanspruchung – für den Betrachter unsichtbar – durch eine Festigkeitssteigerung der verwendeten Materialen angepaßt werden. In den ersten zwei Bürogeschossen über der Eingangshalle sind einzelne Stützen am Übergang zwischen Büro- und Kernbereichen so hoch ausgenutzt, daß zusätzlich zum hochfesten Beton Stahlkerne (Ø 200 mm) eingebaut werden mußten (Bild 5, 6). Rechnerisch mußte für diese einzelnen Stützen aufgrund fehlender Normung für die Kombination von hochfestem Beton mit einbetoniertem Stahlteil ein Normalbeton der Festigkeitsklasse B 55 angenommen werden.

Wegen der deutlich höheren Festigkeit des Betons der Stützen gegenüber dem Beton der Geschoßdecken bedurfte der Anschluß Stütze / Decke besonderer Beachtung. Die übliche Vorgehensweise, die Stützen bis Unterkannte Decke zu betonieren und dann die Decke herzustellen, sollte möglichst beibehalten werden. Dazu wurden beim Betonieren der Decken gleichzeitig zwei Betone unterschiedlicher Festigkeit angeliefert und eingebaut. Der Deckenbeton im Stützenbereich mußte – wie der Stützenbeton – hochfest sein (B 95). Die übrige Decke wurde in Normalbetonqualität (B 45) hergestellt.

Die Verwendung von hochfestem Beton oder – zutreffender ausgedrückt – von Hochleistungsbeton steckt in Deutschland, im Gegensatz zu den USA oder den nordischen Ländern Europas, noch in den Kinderschuhen. Ein Grund dafür wurde bei diesem Neubau offenkundig. Die bürokratischen Hürden in Deutschland sind – wenn bisher nicht genormte Baustoffe über das Einholen einer Zustimmung im Einzelfall verwendet werden sollen – kaum oder nur schwer in der zur Verfügung stehenden Zeit zu überwinden. Ferner ist der geforderte Überwachungsaufwand für solche Baustoffe enorm hoch und verteuert somit ihre Anwendung. Trotz dieser bekannten Schwierigkeiten erwies sich der ausgeschriebene Hochleistungsbeton für

dieses Bauvorhaben als konkurrenzfähig. Nur ein Bieter schlug an Stelle der Stützen aus hochfestem Beton generell Verbundstützen (Stahlbetonstützen aus Normalbeton mit einbetonierten Baustahlprofilen) vor.

Das Arbeiten mit hochfestem Beton ist erst seit den 70er Jahren nach Entwicklung von leistungsfähigen Fließmitteln möglich, da der Wasserzementwert (das Gewichtsverhältnis von Wasser zu Zement) bei den hochfesten Betonen sehr gering sein muß und der Beton deshalb ohne Fließmittel nicht mehr verarbeitet werden kann. Der Wasserzementwert bei hochfesten Betonen liegt zwischen ca. 0,22 und 0,35. Bei Normalbetonen sind dagegen Werte von ca. 0,40 bis etwa 0,65 üblich und je nach Betonierbedingungen weitgehend ohne Fließmittel zu verarbeiten. Als geeigneter Betonzusatzstoff zu signifikantem Verbessern der Kornstruktur wurde zusätzlich der Silicatstaub (Nebenprodukt bei der Ferro-Silicium-Produktion) entdeckt; so wurden mit diesen beiden Produkten enorme Fortschritte in der Betontechnologie möglich.

Gründung

Das gesamte Untergeschoß ist so ausgebildet, daß es als ein steifer Gründungskörper wirken kann. Für die eigentliche Lastübertragung in den Baugrund wurden die beiden klassischen Gründungsvarianten kombiniert. Eine Flachgründung wird an hoch beanspruchten Stellen durch Bohrpfähle ergänzt bzw. ertüchtigt (Bild 7). Die so entstehende Kombination aus Flach- und Pfahlgründung verläßt zwar den durch die derzeit gültigen Normen gesteckten Rahmen, konnte hier jedoch über entsprechende Bodengutachten durchgesetzt werden.

Diese Gründungsvariante war aus statischer und bodenmechanischer Sicht in der hier anstehenden Bodensituation äußerst zweckmäßig und auch wirtschaftlich. Im Gründungsbereich des Neubaus steht eine ca. 10 m mächtige, eiszeitlich vorbelastete Tonschicht an, die Bodenpressungen in der Größenordnung von ca. 200 kN/m² ohne

nennenswerte Setzungen aufnehmen kann. Nur dort wurden zusätzlich Bohrpfähle angeordnet, wo sich infolge der ständigen Lasten ohne solche Bohrpfähle rechnerisch höhere Bodenpressungen ergaben. Die Bohrpfähle durchstoßen die Tonschicht und binden in einer ca. 2 bis 3 m mächtigen Feinsandschicht ein, der Schichten aus Mittel- und Grobsand sowie Geschiebelehme und -tone folgen.

Das mechanische Verhalten der Tonschicht ist dadurch gekennzeichnet, daß sie sich bis zu einer Beanspruchung, die der eiszeitlichen Vorbelastung entspricht, kaum verformt. Die sogenannte Konsolidierung – d.h. das setzungsauslösende Austreten des in den Tonporen gebundenen Wassers infolge Belastung – ist bis zu einer der vorzeitlichen Eisauflast entsprechenden Bodenpressung abgeschlossen. Treten höhere Bodenpressungen auf, beginnt erneut eine Phase der Konsolidierung und der damit verbundenen Setzungen im Ton. Der Ton entzieht sich also dieser Überlast, und die Bohrpfähle übernehmen einen entsprechenden Lastanteil. Diese Art der Gründung ist auch deshalb sehr wirtschaftlich, weil eine Begrenzung der Pfahllasten durch die sogenannte äußere Pfahltragfähigkeit – nachzuweisen über Spitzendruck und Mantelreibung – hier keinen Sinn macht und damit nur die durch den Beton bzw. durch die Bewehrung bestimmte innere Pfahltragfähigkeit maßgebend ist. Dies wird klar, wenn man bedenkt, daß sich die Pfahlsetzungen dem Setzungsverhalten des Bodens anpassen sollen, um überhaupt eine Wechselwirkung zwischen den Bodenpressungen und den Pfahlkräften zu erzielen.

Bei nur kurz andauernden Belastungen, zum Beispiel windbedingten hohen Bodenpressungen an den Rändern des Gründungskörpers, verhält sich der anstehende Ton ebenfalls sehr gutmütig. Setzungen treten dabei praktisch nicht auf, da sie nur infolge Konsolidierung entstehen, diese aber erst nach längerer Lasteinwirkung einsetzt. Damit bedurfte es keiner zusätzlichen Bohrpfähle für Lastfälle mit Windeinwirkung.

8

stage, of course. It was thus possible to adapt the columns to the increasing loading from top to bottom – not visible to the observer – by increasing the strength of the materials used. On the first two office levels above the entrance hall at the transition between the office and core areas, the load-bearing capacity of certain columns is exploited to such a degree that in addition to using high-strength concrete, steel cores 200 mm in diameter had to be built in (ill. 5). In calculating these special columns, the use of normal concrete (B 55) had to be assumed in the absence of any recognized standards for the combination of high-strength concrete and cast-in steel sections.

In view of the considerably higher strength of the concrete in the columns compared with that used in the floor slabs, the abutments between these two elements required special attention. The usual procedure of concreting the columns up to the soffit and then casting the slab itself was to be retained as far as possible. For that reason, two different strengths of concrete were delivered to the site and used simultaneously when pouring the floor slabs. High-strength concrete (B 95 – the same as that in the columns) had to be used for the areas of the floors around the column heads. The remaining areas of the slabs were executed in a normal quality of concrete (B 45).

In contrast to the US and Scandinavian countries, in Germany the use of high-strength – or high-performance – concrete is still in its infancy. One reason for this became apparent in the course of realizing this new structure. In Germany, if one wishes to use materials that are not covered by national standards or where special permission is required for their use in certain situations, it is scarcely possible to overcome the bureaucratic obstacles in the time available. In addition, the supervision required for the use of such materials is enormously expensive and thus increases the construction costs. Nevertheless, in spite of these difficulties, the high-strength concrete specified for

this project proved to be a competitive solution. Only one tenderer suggested executing the columns in a composite form of construction (reinforced concrete, using normal concrete with steel sections cast in) instead of in high-strength concrete.

Only since the 1970s, when efficient super-plasticizers were developed, has it been possible to work with high-strength concrete. This is because the water-cement ratio for this material (the proportion of water to cement by weight) has to be very low; on the other hand, the concrete cannot be worked without plasticizers. The water-cement ratio for high-strength concrete is between roughly 0.22 and 0.35. With normal forms of concrete, values of 0.40 to 0.65 are common, and the material can usually be worked without plasticizers. Silicate powder was also discovered as a suitable additive that considerably improves the grain structure of the concrete. (The powder is a by-product of ferro-silicon production.) Both these products have allowed tremendous advances to be made in concrete technology.

Foundations

The entire basement is constructed to act as a rigid foundation volume. The transmission of loads to the ground was achieved by a combination of the two classical foundation forms: a flat slab is complemented by bored piles at those points subject to particularly heavy loading (ill. 7). This combination does not fall within the accepted scope of current building standards. Nevertheless, it was possible to implement it here on the strength of appropriate soil investigations.

In terms of the structural engineering and soil mechanics, this form of foundation construction proved to be extremely practical and economical in the context of the soil conditions on site. The ground beneath the foundations of the new structure consists of a roughly 10-metre-thick bed of heavy clay compressed during the Ice Age and capable of supporting compression loads of roughly

200 kN/m^2 without any significant settlement. For this reason, additional bored piles were specified only at those points where the permanent loads would have exceeded this pressure on the ground. The bored piles penetrate the bed of clay and are consolidated in a heavy layer of fine sand some two to three metres thick, beneath which are layers of medium and coarse sand as well as boulder clay and till.

In terms of its mechanical behaviour, the clay layer is scarcely subject to deformation before the level of the Ice Age loading is reached. The process of so-called "consolidation" – the escape of the water trapped in the pores of the clay under loading, which results in settlement – has been concluded up to the level of ground compression that occurred during the Ice Age. If greater compression loads were imposed, a new phase of consolidation would begin, accompanied by the phenomenon of settlement in the clay. The clay is not subject to excess loading, since the bored piles bear a commensurate proportion of the loads. This kind of foundation is also very economical, since a limitation of the pile loads by the so-called outer pile load-bearing capacity – determined by means of peak pressure and skin friction – would be pointless here. Only the inner load-bearing capacity of the pile is relevant, determined by the type of concrete and reinforcement used. This becomes clear if one considers that the pile settlement should be matched to the settlement behaviour of the ground in order to achieve a correlation between soil compression and the pile forces.

In the case of short-term loading – for example, high pressures on the ground at the edges of the foundation structure caused by wind – the clay reacts in a benevolent manner. There is virtually no settlement, since this occurs as a result of consolidation; and consolidation manifests itself only after a longer period of loading. As a result, no additional bored piles were necessary for loads resulting from the action of wind.

Das Entstehen des Gebäudes

Construction of the Building

1 Blick über die Halle 26 zum Verwaltungsgebäude
während der Bauzeit
2 Anschlußbewehrung der aussteifenden Wände
im Erschließungsturm
3 Bewehrung der Flachdecke im Randbereich
mit Kopfbolzendübeln
zur Sicherung gegen Durchstanzen
4 Deckenbewehrung im Stützenbereich
mit Absperrgitter für den Einbau von zwei Betonsorten
5 Bewehrung der Betonplatte in der von Spundwänden
umschlossenen Baugrube

1 View over Hall 26 to administration tower
during construction
2 Reinforcement starter bars for bracing walls
in access tower
3 Reinforcement to flat slab at edge
with stud shear connectors to prevent punching
4 Reinforcement to floor slab in area around
column head with grating as separation
between two kinds of concrete
5 Reinforcement to base slab in basement excavation
surrounded by sheet piling

1 Spezial-Stützenschalung zum Betonieren
  der Fertigteilstützen in Schräglage
2 Befestigen von Ketten zum Aufrichten
  der Fertigteilstütze mit Stahlkern
3 Fertigteile mit Rohrleitungsführung
  durch die Außenwand im UG
4 Köcher zum Einbringen der Fertigteilstütze.
  Der sich um die Stütze ergebende Raum
  wird vergossen
5 Anschlußbewehrung der trägerrostartigen Wände
  an die Decke über UG
6 Fertigteilstützen mit und ohne massive Stahlkerne

p. 48

1 Special column shuttering for casting
  precast concrete elements in sloping position
2 Fixing chains to hoist precast concrete column with
  steel core
3 Prefabricated elements with tubular sleeves through
  external wall of basement
4 Sleeve for fixing precast concrete column.
  The space around the column is filled with concrete
5 Reinforcement starter bars to box-grid walls
  at level of floor over basement
6 Precast concrete columns with and without
  solid steel cores

1 Anziehen einer Kontermutter im Stoßbereich
2 Holzschablone zum Positionieren
  der Bewehrungsstäbe
3 Einbau einer Wendelbewehrung
4 Fertigteilstützen im EG
5 Blick in den Bewehrungskorb einer Fertigteilstütze
6 Vermessungsarbeiten bei der Bauausführung

1 Tightening a counternut in the area
  of reinforcement joints
2 Wood templet for positioning reinforcement bars
3 Assembly of helical reinforcement
4 Precast concrete columns on ground floor
5 View into reinforcement cage
  of a precast concrete column
6 Surveying work during the construction stage

Das Entstehen des Gebäudes

Construction of the Building

1 Richtfest: Festschmuck aus Bauwerkzeug
2 Kletterschalung am Kopf des nordöstlichen Kerns
3 Südwestlicher Kern, links Halle 18

1 Topping-out ceremony: festive decoration,
  consisting of construction tools
2 Climbing shuttering at the head of the north-east core
3 South-west core with Hall 18 on the left

1 bis 3 Vorfabrikation des Turmaufsatzes
im Stahlbaubetrieb
4 bis 6 Turmaufsatz: Vormontage am Boden

1 to 3 Prefabrication of framed steel tower extension
4 to 6 Tower extension: preassembly on the ground

1 bis 5   Anlieferung und Montage der Teile
des Turmaufsatzes
6 und 7 Aufrichten des Turmaufsatzes am Boden

1 to 5   Delivery and assembly of sections
of tower extension
6 and 7 Hoisting the tower extension
into a vertical position on the ground

4

1

2

5

3

6

7

1 bis 3 Ziehen des Turmaufsatzes durch Schwerlastkran
4 bis 6 Aufsetzen und Befestigen des Turmaufsatzes

1 to 3 Hoisting the tower extension into position
        with a heavy-duty crane
4 to 6 Lowering and fixing the tower extension

1

Thermisches Konzept und Lüftungskonzept

Thermal and Ventilation Concepts

Gerhard Hausladen
Martin Többen

Das realisierte Konzept zur Versorgung des Gebäudes mit Wärme/Kälte und mit Luft ist neuartig hinsichtlich seiner geringen Verbrauchswerte.

The concept for the heating, cooling and ventilation systems as implemented is new in respect of the low energy-consumption values achieved.

Wärme-/Kälte-Management

In den deutschen Arbeitsstätten-Richtlinien sind die Anforderungen an die thermischen Eigenschaften von Büroräumen festgelegt. Die Qualität der thermischen Behaglichkeit im Innenraum wird jedoch allein über das Erreichen und Sicherstellen einer vorgegebenen Lufttemperatur nur unzureichend definiert. Ergänzend zu den Forderungen aus den erwähnten Richtlinien sind nämlich folgende Faktoren für das Wohlbefinden von Bedeutung:
- die empfundene Raumtemperatur,
- die Symmetrie der Oberflächen-temperaturen,
- die individuelle Einflußnahme des Nutzers,
- der Ausgleich von Lastschwankungen.

Heating and cooling management

Thermal requirements for offices are set out in the German code of practice for workplaces. But defining the quality of thermal comfort solely in terms of achieving and maintaining a predetermined room temperature is not sufficient in itself. In addition to the requirements contained in the code of practice, the following factors are important for a sense of well-being:
- the perceived room temperature
- the symmetry of surface temperatures
- the individual influence exerted by the user
- balancing out load fluctuations.

Energieform und Lastverhalten

Durch Ermitteln der dynamischen Lastverläufe in einer Simulation läßt sich ableiten, welche Energieform (Wärme/Kälte) dem Gebäude zugeführt werden muß. Gebäude mit gutem Dämmstandard haben einen geringen Wärmebedarf. Oft reichen bei Neubauten, die heutigen Dämmstandards entsprechen, interne Wärmegewinne (Personen, Geräte, Kunstlicht) aus, um ein Gebäude zu weiten Teilen der Nutzungszeit zu beheizen. Bereits ab Außentemperaturen von etwa 0 °C aufwärts sind Räume mit hohen internen Wärmegewinnen zu kühlen. Deshalb ist die maßgebliche Energieform die Kühlenergie; das Erzeugen von Kühlenergie ist wesentlich aufwendiger als das von Wärmeenergie. Das Energieversorgungskonzept ist darauf ausgelegt, ressourcenschonend zu kühlen. Der zum Beheizen erforderliche Restwärmebedarf spielt eine untergeordnete Rolle; die hierfür benötigte Energie dient nur dazu, das Gebäude während der ungenutzten Zeit (Nacht, Wochenende) nicht auskühlen zu lassen.

Forms of energy and load behaviour

The form of energy (heating/cooling) required in a building can be established after determining the dynamic load patterns in a simulation. Buildings with a good level of insulation in the outer skins have low heating needs. In new buildings that comply with modern insulation standards, internal heat gains (from people, appliances, artificial lighting, etc.) are often adequate to heat the building for much of the time it is in use. With external temperatures of 0 °C and above, rooms with large internal heat gains will actually require cooling. The decisive form of energy in that case will be cooling energy. It is a well-known fact, however, that the generation of cooling energy is considerably more expensive than producing heating energy. The energy supply concept for the present building is conceived on the basis of cooling with a minimum exploitation of resources. In comparison, the residual thermal needs for heating play a subordinate role. The energy required for this purpose is used merely to prevent the building from cooling out during the time it is not in use (at night, over the weekend, etc.).

1 und 2 Büroraum: Innere Fassade mit natürlicher
        und künstlicher Belüftung;
        Lüftungsaustritt im Sockelbereich
3   Blick in den Zwischentemperaturbereich
        der Korridorfassade

1 and 2 Office: inner facade layer with provision
        for natural and artificial ventilation;
        air supply in apron wall
3   View into intermediate temperature zone
        of corridor facade

Hybride Lüftung

Jedes zweite Fassadenfeld enthält ein zu öffnendes Schiebefenster (2,0 x 1,0 m). Im Brüstungsbereich ist ein Zuluftauslaß eingefügt, der bei geschlossenem Fenster die Lüftungsfunktion übernimmt. Mit Hilfe einer mechanischen Verbindung (Bowdenzug) wird dieser beim Öffnen des Schiebefensters geschlossen (wahlweise natürliche oder mechanische Lüftung). Die Abluft wird mit Hilfe eines zentralen Kanalsystems über einen Rotations-Wärmetauscher oben aus dem Gebäude geführt.

Doppelfassade

Der Korridor der Doppelfassade wird mit unterschiedlichen Luftmengen durchströmt. Als Antrieb dient dabei die Windkraft. Während der kalten Jahreszeit soll die Fassadenkonstruktion möglichst wenig auskühlen, um die Transmission zu reduzieren. Daher wird die eintretende Luftmenge auf ein Mindestmaß beschränkt. Im Sommer wird einfallende Strahlungswärme mit hohen Luftvolumenströmen abgeführt. Die horizontale Durchlüftung der Doppelfassade wird durch verstellbare Klappen reguliert.

Die physikalischen Grundsätze der Gebäude-Aerodynamik zeigen, vereinfacht dargestellt, daß an einer dem Wind zugewandten Fassadenseite positiver Druck vorherrscht und auf der windabgewandten Seite negativer Druck zu erwarten ist. Dieses Druckgefälle wird mit Hilfe von Zu- und Abluftklappen, die in der Außenhaut der Doppelfassade angeordnet sind, abgepuffert. Das jeweilige Öffnungsmaß der Fassadenklappen wird nach den im Windkanal ermittelten Druckverhältnissen, abhängig von der Windrichtung, der Windgeschwindigkeit und der Außentemperatur eingestellt.

Dem Nutzer stehen wahlweise zwei Systeme mit unterschiedlichem Angebot zur Verfügung: Im Winter bietet die natürliche Lüftung aus der Doppelfassade, bzw. dem kontrollierten Doppelraum kühlere Luft, während das mechanische System wärmere Luft

Hybrid forms of ventilation

Every second facade bay contains a sliding window (2.0 x 1.0 m). Incorporated in the apron panels are air inlets that provide a further means of ventilation when the windows are closed. A mechanical device connected to the casements (Bowden element) closes the air inlets when the sliding windows are opened. In this way a choice is allowed between natural and mechanical forms of ventilation. Vitiated air is removed via a central duct system and conducted over a rotary heat-exchange unit before being discharged from the building.

Two-layer facade

The volume of air flowing through the corridor space between the two facade layers varies. The circulation is maintained by wind power. In order to reduce thermal transmission, the two-layer facade should be allowed to cool out as little as possible during the cold season. The volume of air entering this space is, therefore, kept to a minimum at that time of year. In summer, solar heat is removed by an increased volume of air flowing through the corridor. Horizontal ventilation of the facade space is regulated by adjustable flaps.

Expressed in simple terms, the laws of aerodynamics for buildings show that positive pressure prevails on the facade facing the wind, while negative pressure may be expected on the leeward side. In the present building, this pressure gradient is brought into a state of equilibrium by means of air inlet and outlet flaps in the outer skin of the two-layer facade. The dimensions of the individual flap openings, which depend on the direction and velocity of the wind and the external temperature, were determined on the basis of pressure conditions calculated in wind-tunnel tests.

Users have a choice between two systems. In winter, the natural ventilation system via the two-layer facade – the conditioned buffer zone – offers cooler air, while the

1 Thermoaktive Decke
   Schema der Heiz- und Kühlleitungen, Regelgeschosse,
   Maßstab 1:250

   1 Vertikaltrasse Heiz- und Kühlleitungen
   2 Verlegemuster der Rohrleitungen, auf die flexible
     Anforderung der Bürotrennwände abgestimmt
   3 Unterflurkanal, Elektro-
     und Kommunikationsleitungen
   4 Elektrotrassen, Anschluß
     in regelmäßigen Abständen (1,80 m)

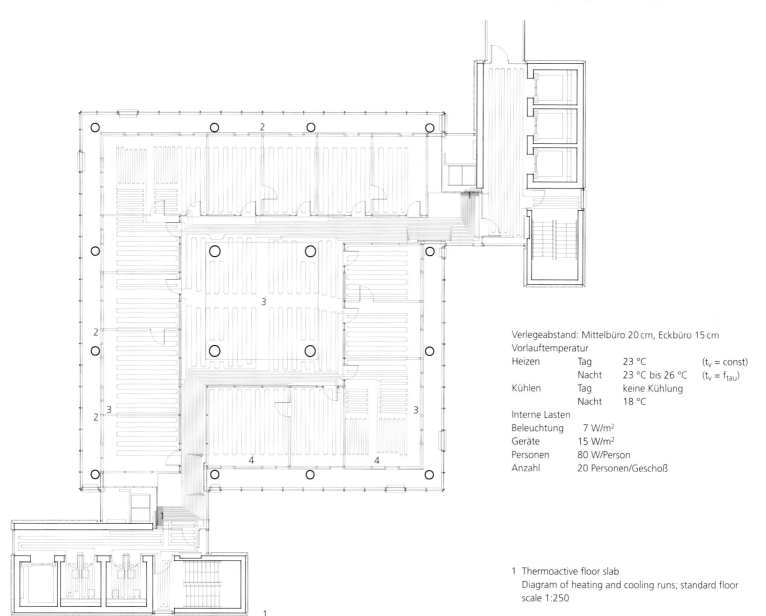

1

Verlegeabstand: Mittelbüro 20 cm, Eckbüro 15 cm
Vorlauftemperatur

Heizen	Tag	23 °C	(t_v = const)
	Nacht	23 °C bis 26 °C	($t_v = f_{tau}$)
Kühlen	Tag	keine Kühlung	
	Nacht	18 °C	

Interne Lasten
Beleuchtung   7 W/m²
Geräte   15 W/m²
Personen   80 W/Person
Anzahl   20 Personen/Geschoß

1 Thermoactive floor slab
   Diagram of heating and cooling runs; standard floor
   scale 1:250

   1 Vertical heating and cooling runs
   2 Pipe distribution layout, allowing for office partitions
     to be moved
   3 Subfloor duct for electrical and communications runs
   4 Electrical line connections at fixed centres (1.80 m)

Spacing of coils: central office 20 cm;
corner office 15 cm
Flow temperature

Heating:	day	23 °C	(flow temp. = constant)
	night	23 °C	
		to 26 °C	(flow temp. = f/ext. temp.)
Cooling:	day	no cooling	
	night	18 °C	

Internal loads:
lighting   7 W/m²
equipment   15 W/m²
people   80 W/person
no. of persons 20 per floor

zur Verfügung stellt; im Sommer ist dies umgekehrt. Dieses Prinzip gilt auch während der Übergangszeiten, so daß sich der Nutzer durch die Wahl der Lufttemperatur seine individuelle Raumkondition einstellen kann.

Thermoaktive Decke
Die thermische Aktivierung einer massiven Decke ist mit wasserdurchströmten Rohrleitungen möglich. Auf der Deckenkonstruktion werden im Estrich Rohre ähnlich einer Fuß-

mechanical system supplies warmer air. In summer, the system is reversed. The same principle applies during transitional periods as well, so that users can regulate their own spatial conditions through the choice of air temperature.

Thermoactive floor slab
A solid floor slab can be thermally activated by means of water-bearing pipes. These are laid in the screed over the floor structure rather like the runs of an underfloor

2 bis 4 Thermoaktive Decke, Bauzeit

2 to 4 Thermoactive floor slab during construction

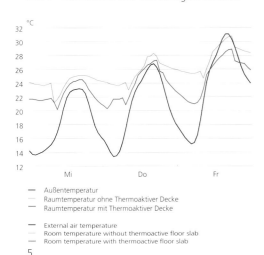

— Außentemperatur
— Raumtemperatur ohne Thermoaktiver Decke
— Raumtemperatur mit Thermoaktiver Decke

— External air temperature
— Room temperature without thermoactive floor slab
— Room temperature with thermoactive floor slab

5

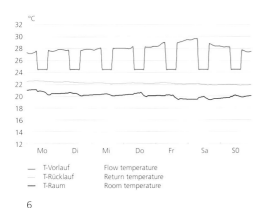

— T-Vorlauf   Flow temperature
— T-Rücklauf   Return temperature
— T-Raum   Room temperature

6

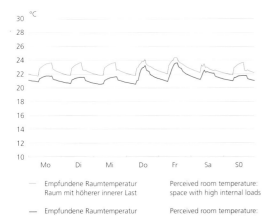

— Empfundene Raumtemperatur   Perceived room temperature:
  Raum mit höherer innerer Last   space with high internal loads

— Empfundene Raumtemperatur   Perceived room temperature:
  Raum mit niedriger innerer Last   space with low internal loads

7

bodenheizung verlegt. Um vergleichbare Wärme- und Kälteströme nach oben und unten zu leiten, wird auf eine Dämmlage (Trittschalldämmung) verzichtet. Gleichzeitiges Temperieren von Decke und Fußboden läßt zwei thermisch aktive Oberflächen entstehen.

So wird zwischen allen Geschossen – im Gegensatz zu einer Fußbodenheizung – eine in jedem Raum doppelt wirksame Fläche geschaffen; sie hat eine enorme Verringerung der nötigen Temperaturdifferenz zwischen Raumtemperatur und aktiver Oberflächentemperatur zur Folge.

Zum Abdecken von Wärmelasten (t außen < 0 °C) ist eine Oberflächentemperatur von ca. 23 °C erforderlich. Bei Raumtemperaturen unter 23 °C beginnt der Heizbetrieb. Analog dazu sind im Kühlbetrieb (t außen > 0 °C) Oberflächentemperaturen von 21 °C erforderlich; bei Raumtemperaturen über 21 °C kühlt also die Thermoaktive Decke durch sehr geringe Temperaturdifferenzen den Raum.

Ausgewählte Ergebnisse der Simulation

Die im folgenden dargestellten Ergebnisse einer dynamischen Simulation zeigen das Verhalten der Thermoaktiven Decke:
• Sommerliches Verhalten
  5 Im Vergleich zu einem ungekühlten Raum zeigt sich beim Betrieb der Thermoaktiven Decke eine um bis zu 3 °K geringere Raumtemperatur.
• Winterliches Verhalten
  6 Für einen Nord/West-Raum ist eine kalte Winterwoche ohne Belegung und ohne interne Lasten dargestellt. Es zeigt sich, daß die Raumtemperatur nicht unter 20 °C sinkt.
• Räume mit unterschiedlicher interner Last
  7 Für zwei nebeneinanderliegende Räume wird der Temperaturverlauf bei unterschiedlichen inneren Lasten dargestellt. Raum 1 hat keine Belegung; Raum 2 ist überbelegt.

heating installation. In order to obtain a comparable flow of heating and cooling streams upwards and downwards, the usual acoustic insulation layer is omitted. The simultaneous heating of the floor and the ceiling means that two thermally active surfaces are created.

In this way, in contrast to normal underfloor heating systems, two thermally effective surfaces exist between storeys in every room. This results in a huge reduction of the required difference between room temperature and active surface temperature.

To cover heating loads (external temp. < 0 °C), a surface temperature of approximately 23 °C is necessary. When room temperatures sink below 23 °C, therefore, the heating system comes into operation. Conversely, for cooling operations (external temp. > 0 °C), a surface temperature of 21 °C is necessary. When the room temperature exceeds 21 °C, the thermoactive floor cools the room by means of extremely small temperature differences.

Selected simulation data

The results of a dynamic simulation given below show the behaviour of the thermoactive floor slab.
• Behaviour in summer
  5 When the thermoactive floor slab is in operation, the room temperature will be up to about 3 °K lower than that in an uncooled room.
• Behaviour in winter
  6 The data shown is for an unoccupied north- or west-facing room without internal loads during a cold week in winter. The room temperature does not sink below 20 °C.
• Rooms with varying internal loads
  7 The temperature range is shown for two adjoining rooms with different internal loads. Room 1 is unoccupied. Room 2 is crowded.

Ressourcenschonende Kühlung

Das Konzept einer ressourcenschonenden Kühlung greift auf das vorhandene Kälte-potential der niederen Nachttemperaturen zurück. Um die bis zu 15 °K kühlere Nachtluft am folgenden Tag nutzen zu können, muß die Kälte zwischengespeichert werden. Als thermisches Speichermedium bietet sich das Gebäudetragwerk an, speziell die Geschoß-decken aus Beton sind hier geeignet.

Rückkühlung

Die Kühle der Nachtluft wird mit Hilfe eines Hybridkühlers an einen Wasserkreislauf über-tragen. Mit seiner Hilfe kann zusätzlich die Verdampfungswärme von Wasser, welches auf die Kühlelemente aufgesprüht wird, genutzt werden. So ist auch in warmen Som-mernächten eine Kühlwassertemperatur bis zu 18 °C zu erreichen. Der Hybridkühler wird im Sommer und in der Übergangszeit in zwei unterschiedlichen Betriebsweisen eingesetzt. Für den Betrieb der Thermoaktiven Decke liefert der Hybridkühler in der Nacht ein Tem-peraturniveau von ca. 18 °C. Am Tag arbeitet das Rückkühlwerk für die Kältemaschine.

Die erzeugte mechanische Kälte wird zum Kühlen von Sonderräumen (»Hermes-Lounge« und technische Betriebsräume) verwendet.

Mechanische Be- und Entlüftungsanlage

Die Außenluft für alle Regelgeschosse ein-schließlich der Vorstandsetage wird im Dach-bereich des nördlichen Erschließungsturms angesaugt. Das Vorwärmen geschieht mit Hilfe eines Rotations-Wärmetauschers, der bis zu 85 % des Energieinhalts der Abluft zurückgewinnt. Nach der Luftaufbereitung (Heizen/Kühlen) im Technikgeschoß wird die Zuluft in zwei großformatige Schächte einge-speist. Diese versorgen jedes Regelgeschoß mit einer maximalen Luftmenge von 2000 m³/h, was einem 1,5-fachen Luftwech-sel entspricht. Die tatsächlich verwendete Luftmenge bestimmt sich anhand des hygie-nisch erforderlichen Luftaustausches, der mit Hilfe von CO_2-Sensoren und einer ersten

Cooling without wasting resources

The concept of cooling without wasting resources implies exploiting the potential of lower night-time temperatures. In order to use the night air, which is up to 15 °K cooler, it is necessary to store it until the following day. The structural members of the building – especially the concrete floor slabs – are an ideal thermal storage medium.

Recooling

The cooling energy of the night air is trans-ferred to a water circulation system by means of a hybrid cooling plant. This plant can also be used to exploit the evaporative heat of water sprayed on to the cooling elements. In this way, during warm summer nights, a cooling-water temperature of up to 18 °C can be achieved. The hybrid cooling plant is operated in summer and in the transitional seasons in two different forms. At night, it maintains a temperature level of roughly 18 °C in the thermoactive floor slabs. During the day, the recooling plant is operated in place of the cooling plant. The mechanical cooling energy generated is used for cooling special spaces such as the Hermes Lounge and technical services rooms.

Mechanical ventilation

The fresh-air supply for all standard floors, including the executive level, is sucked into the northern core structure at roof level. The air is preheated with the aid of a rotary heat-exchange unit that recovers up to 85 per cent of the energy content from discharged exhaust air. After the process of air condi-tioning (heating/cooling) on the services floor, the air intake is fed into two large shafts. These supply each of the standard floors with a maximum of 2,000 cubic metres of air per hour – equivalent to an air exchange rate of 1.5. The actual volume of air supplied is determined on the basis of the air exchange rate required to maintain hygienic conditions. This reflects initial expe-

1 und 2 Hybridkühler unter der Dachterrasse
3 Blick in die Technikzentrale

1 and 2 Hybrid cooling element beneath roof terrace
3 View into mechanical services centre

Nutzererfahrung während des Betriebes fein-eingestellt wurde. Die Luftmenge dient nicht dem Ausgleich von Heiz- oder Kühllasten. Die Abluft wird analog zur Zuluft in zwei Schächten geführt, die im oberen Technikge-schoß zusammenlaufen. Dem Luftaustausch je Geschoß dienen elektrisch betriebene Volumenstromregler für Zu- und Abluft. Um möglichst geringe Druckverluste im Kanal-netz zu gewährleisten, sind die Zu- und Abluftkanäle für eine Luftgeschwindigkeit von 1,0 bis 2,0 Meter pro Sekunde (m/s) dimensioniert. Innerhalb der zentralen und gradlinigen Steigschächte stellen sich Luft-geschwindigkeiten von bis 4,0 m/s ein. Ober-halb des nördlichen Erschließungsturms sind Ventilatoren mit freilaufenden Rädern ange-ordnet, die unterstützt von natürlichen Kräf-ten (Auftrieb, Wind) die Luftförderung gewährleisten. Die Fortluft wird an der obe-ren Gebäudespitze nach außen geführt. Auf-grund der geringen Druckverluste, des ther-mischen Auftriebs sowie der zu erwartenden Unterstützung durch Windkräfte wird die Luftbewegung im Gebäude zu weiten Teilen natürlich unterstützt, was eine Reduzierung der Ventilatorlaufzeiten zur Folge hat.

Zusammenfassung

Die natürliche Lüftung über das Schiebefen-ster ist ein elementares Prinzip im Rahmen des Lüftungskonzeptes. Die störenden Ein-flüsse aus Wind und Wetter werden mit Hilfe der Doppelfassade sowie des inneren (mechanischen) Lüftungssystemes kompen-siert. Der wesentliche Anteil des Wärme-bedarfs wird aus der Abluft über die Wärme-rückgewinnungsanlage mit dem hocheffizi-enten Rotations-Wärmetauscher gedeckt. So kommt ein weitgehend natürliches Lüftungs-konzept zustande, welches, mechanisch unterstützt, mit einem nur geringen Auf-wand an Primärenergie betrieben wird.

rience of user needs and can be finely adjusted during operation with the aid of CO_2 sensors. The volume of air does not serve to balance heating or cooling loads. Like the air intake, the air extract is drawn through two shafts, which merge in the ser-vices storey at the top of the building. The air exchange rate for each storey is controlled by electrically operated volume-flow regulators for the air intake and extract. In order to minimize the loss of pressure in the ducting network, the air supply and extract ducts are dimensioned for an air velocity of 1.0 to 2.0 metres per second (m/s). Within the straight-line central riser shafts, air velocities of up to 4.0 m/s occur. Fans with free-running rotors are installed above the northern core struc-ture. These maintain the air circulation with the support of natural forces (thermal uplift and wind). Vitiated air is discharged at the top of the building. As a result of the rela-tively small pressure losses, the thermal uplift and the anticipated support of wind currents, air circulation within the building is main-tained largely by natural means. This, in turn, reduces the operating time of the fans.

Summary

Natural ventilation via sliding windows forms a fundamental principle of the ventila-tion concept. The disturbing effects of wind and weather are offset by the two-layer facade construction and the internal (mechanical) ventilation system. Heating needs are met largely by the energy recov-ered from exhaust air. The heat-recovery plant incorporates a highly efficient rotary heat-exchange unit. As a result, it was possi-ble to achieve a largely natural system of ventilation, which, with mechanical support, can be operated with only a small consump-tion of primary energy.

Inneneinrichtung

Interior Design

1 Büroraum
2 Flur im Regelgeschoß
3 Mittelzone im Regelgeschoß
4 Cafeteria
5 Geländer-Detail im Treppenhaus
6 Waschtisch im Sanitärraum
7 Besprechungsraum in der Hermes-Lounge
8 Decken-Untersicht in der Eingangshalle
9 Eingangshalle
10 Hermes-Lounge

3

1

4

2

5

6

1 Office
2 Corridor on standard floor
3 Central zone on standard floor
4 Cafeteria
5 Staircase balustrade detail
6 Washbasin unit in sanitary area
7 Discussion room in Hermes Lounge
8 View of soffit over entrance hall
9 Entrance hall
10 Hermes Lounge

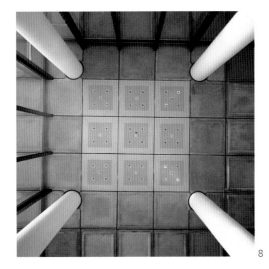

8

7

9

10

Gebäudedaten

Geschosse	20
Länge x Breite	35,1 x 37,5 m
Höhe nördlicher Erschließungsturm	82 m
max. Höhe über alles	ca. 110 m
Fußboden höchster Aufenhaltsraum	+ 58,32 m
Bruttogrundrißfläche	13.563 m²
Bruttorauminhalt	48.181 m³
Grundfläche Büroturm	24 x 24 m
Fassaden	10.500 m²
Hüllfläche gesamt	12.520 m²
Arbeitsplätze gesamt	ca. 250
Baubeginn	Sommer 1997
Inbetriebnahme	Frühjahr 1999

Baukosten
ca. DM 3.900 / m²

Betriebskosten (errechnet)
ca. DM 12,50 / m²
bei erforderlichen Energieverbrauchern
(Pumpen, Ventilatoren, Aufzüge,
Beleuchtung, Heizung, Kühlung)
Vergleich zu ähnlichen Gebäuden
mit konventioneller Technik — ca. DM 15.– bis 38.– / m²

Doppelfassade
- 2 x k-Wert Glas, 1,1 W / m² / K
- Fensterlüftung über Doppelfassade möglich
  Nutzen des Solareintrags in Doppelfassade zur Luftvorwärmung
- Horizontale Luftbewegung von Süd- auf Nordseite
  mit Ventilatoren
- Nutzen der passiven solaren Überschüsse der Südseite
  auf der Nordseite

Lüftung
- Maximale mechanische Luftwechselrate — 1,5 / h
- Luftwechsel CO_2-geregelt

Heizen und Kühlen
- Bauteiltemperierung
  in den Geschoßdecken
- Freie Kühlung während der Nacht (Hybridkühler)

Spezifischer Jahresheizwärmebedarf
< 50 kWh / m²
- 43 kWh / m² / a (errechnet)
- Unterschreitung der Anforderung um ca. 25%
  (Niedrigenergiehaus-Standard)

Construction Data

No. of storeys	20
Length x width	35.1 x 37.5 m
Height of northern core	82 m
Max. overall height	approx. 110 m
Floor level of highest occupied space	+ 58.32 m
Gross storey area	13,563 m²
Gross volume	48,181 m³
Office tower	24 x 24 m
Facades	10,500 m²
Total area of outer skin	12,520 m²
No. of workplaces	approx. 250
Commencement of construction	summer 1997
Taken into service	spring 1999

Construction costs
approx. DM 3,900 / m²

Operating costs (estimated)
approx. DM 12.50 / m²
for necessary energy-using plant
(pumps, fans, lifts,
lighting, heating, cooling)
Operating costs of comparable buildings
with conventional technology — approx. DM 15.– to 38.– / m²

Two-layer facade
- 2 x U-value glass 1.1 W / m² / K
- window ventilation possible via two-layer facade
- use of solar gains in two-layer facade for preheating air
- horizontal airflow from south to north side
  with use of fans
- use of passive solar energy excess from south side
  on north side

Ventilation
- maximum mechanical air-exchange rate — 1.5 / h
- air exchange, CO_2 regulated

Heating and cooling
- heating and cooling of building via thermal activation
  of structural elements
- free cooling at night (hybrid cooling system)

Specific annual heating needs
< 50 kWh / m²
- 43 kWh / m² / a (estimated)
- approx. 25% reduction of requirements achieved
  (low-energy building standard)

© Prestel Verlag Munich · London · New York
and Herzog + Partner Munich

Die Deutsche Bibliothek – CIP-Einheitsaufnahme
Nachhaltige Höhe : Verwaltungshochhaus
Deutsche Messe AG Hannover / Hrsg.: Thomas Herzog ·
München : Prestel, 2000
ISBN 3-7913-2295-8

Prestel books are available worldwide. Please contact
your nearest bookseller or write to either
of the following addresses for information concerning
your local distributor:

Prestel Verlag
Mandlstrasse 26, 80802 Munich, Germany
Phone +49 (089) 38 17 09-0, Fax +49 (089) 38 17 09-35;
16 West 22nd Street, New York, NY 10010 USA
Phone +1 (212) 627-9090, Fax +1 (212) 627-9511;
and 4 Bloomsbury Place, London WC1A 2QA
Phone +44 (0171) 323 5004, Fax +44 (0171) 636 8004

Design and co-ordination: Verena Herzog-Loibl
and Johannes Determann
Translation: Peter Green
Offset lithography: MedienService, Brodschelm, Munich
Composition: Max Vornehm GmbH, Munich
Printing and Binding: Aumüller Druck KG, Regensburg

Printed in Germany
ISBN 3-7913-2295-8

Photo Acknowledgements

Aerophot Demuss	Seite / page 7
Ingo Brosch	Seite 1, 34 (2), 40, 43, 44, 47, 48, 49, 50 (1,2), 52 (2,3), 53 (2,3,5,6), 57 (3,4)
Verena Herzog-Loibl	Seite / page 2, 34 (3), 38 (2,4), 50 (3), 51, 53 (1)
Moritz Korn	Seite / page 34 (1), 35, 52 (1,4,6,7), 54, 55 (3), 58 (2,3)
Dieter Leistner	Umschlag / cover, Seite / page 4/5, 11, 14, 15, 26/27, 37, 39, 60 (2,3,4), 61
Roland Schneider	Seite / page 9, 12, 17, 19, 34 (4,5,6), 36, 38 (3), 46, 52 (5), 53 (4), 60 (1,5,6), 63, 64
Martin Többen	Seite / page 38 (5), 55 (2), 57 (2), 58 (1)

Zeichnungen / drawings

Deutsche Messe AG, Hannover	Seite / page 13
Herzog + Partner Mitarbeiter / assistant: Peter Gotsch	Seite / page 15, 16, 18, 20/21, 22, 23, 24, 25, 30, 31, 32, 33, 38, 56, 57
Modern Tools, Joachim Nicolaus, München	Seite / page 28/29
Sailer Stepan und Partner, München	Seite / page 40, 41, 42, 43, 45

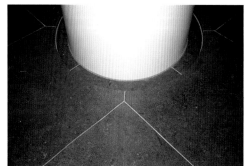